# INFIDELITY sleuth

# INFIDELITY
# sleuth

## A Female Private Eye Tells Women
## How to Uncover the Truth

JULIA HARTLEY MOORE

Ulysses Press

Published by Ulysses Press
        P.O. Box 3440
        Berkeley, CA 94703
        www.ulyssespress.com

ISBN 1-56975-525-6
Library of Congress Control Number 2005908371

Editorial and production staff: Kathryn Brooks, Lily Chou,
    Nicholas Denton-Brown, Lisa Kester
Cover Design: Lourdes Robles
Interior Design: Leslie Henriques, Lourdes Robles

Printed in Canada by Transcontinental Printing

10 9 8 7 6 5 4 3 2 1

Distributed by Publishers Group West

# TABLE OF CONTENTS

Introduction                                             7

1    Dispelling the Myths of Infidelity              17

2    Signs of Betrayal                               44

3    Women Are Their Own Worst Enemies               67

4    Human Nature Is a Curious Thing                 89

5    How to Spot a Cheater from 1000 Yards          111

6    How to Have an Affair                          145

7    A Word to the Guys                             157

8    When You Live with a Liar                      166

9    Women Who Leave                                171

10   Men Are Their Own Worst Enemies                186

11   Most Frequently Asked Questions                194

12   Turn the Wounds into Wisdom                    200


About the Author                                   214

# INTRODUCTION

It doesn't matter how rich, beautiful, powerful, successful or intelligent you are—infidelity doesn't care. Infidelity doesn't discriminate. Infidelity couldn't care less where you live, what you drive, what career path you've chosen, what religion you practice, what your ethnic background is, what gender you are, what your sexual preference is or what political affiliations you have. It can strike at any time with a force so powerful that it renders you incapable of functioning on all cylinders. It contaminates your waking thoughts and makes sleep impossible. In fact, experts tell us that to live with such stress levels for a prolonged period can seriously reduce our life expectancy by 10–14 years. That on its own is reason enough to write this book.

Having read this you would think women facing betrayal would leave their marriages for the sake of their health, well-being and sanity, but, alas, the truth is that 95 percent of women facing betrayal choose to stay in these contaminated relationships.

Hillary Rodham Clinton is a prime example, not because she's rich and famous (infidelity doesn't care) but because she is typical in her responses as a woman betrayed. With all the resources available to her—education, money, social standing and power—she chooses to stay in a marriage where really "The best barometer for the future is the past." Yet in her recent book she states she is "committed to her marriage," which I don't doubt for a moment. However, more importantly, taking the past into account, one would have to ask the question, "Is Bill?" If she answered that question truthfully and considered the rumors (there's no smoke without fire) about his previous dalliances with Paula Jones and Gennifer Flowers, the answer would have to be "No!" And therefore, like so many others, Hillary will live with elements of stress as long as she lives with Bill.

At this stage I think it's important for you to understand where my knowledge and experience comes from. People are intrigued by how a woman with no police background got into the business of private investigation. Let's just say it didn't happen overnight. I can only liken it to an actor or artist who all of a sudden seems to come from nowhere, bursting onto the scene and winning acclaim for their first feature film or exhibition. Everyone is amazed at how lucky they've been to achieve so much so soon but what most people don't realize is that for most of their life they've studied and polished their craft to prepare them for this opportunity. It just so happened that the time had come for them to be brought to the world's attention.

Just like for the actor or artist, it's been a long, slow process for me. My whole life to this point has literally groomed me for this job. Private investigation was the most obvious career choice for me and still is. I get the most incredible sense of fulfillment and joy from my work, knowing I'm doing what I was meant to be doing. I want everyone who has experienced the effects of infidelity to see it as a process of learning and to turn it into something positive instead of dwelling on the negative. I want you to gain the knowledge you need to help you avoid experiencing the pain of your partner's infidelity again, or if you do have to suffer it again, to learn the survival skills to help you understand it and get through it. This is without doubt my true purpose and why I'm so darned good at it.

It takes all sorts to make the world go round and when it comes to infidelity and betrayal there's a saying I think sums up a large percentage of the people I come across: "People are strange." Most people, and especially my clients, think of infidelity and betrayal as purely a heterosexual activity between a man and a woman. But the betrayal of a spouse is often clandestine and secretive and the reason for that is because it's centered on the unexpected, the unusual and the downright kinky, not to mention some behavior most people would find very hard to talk about. Yet if it's happening out there then I've come across it at least twice, and some of the behavior that I would once have considered outlandish has become the norm. Anything from cross-dressing to grown men dressing as babies and having wet nurses to getting your rocks off dressed in a costume (gorilla suits are very popular) are at the "less sinister" end of the spectrum, if you could call it that. All of these practices are done in secret and in many cases come as a complete surprise to the perpetrator's partner or wife.

Honestly, the one aspect of this job that initially shocked me wasn't the guy in the gorilla suit but the number of married men we found participating in homosexual encounters, including a number of professional men who order "sex to go" at lunchtime with rent boys, without ever having to leave their office. This form of behavior is happening everywhere and uncovering it is all in a day's work for my team.

Many of my clients' husbands who indulge in these activities outside of their marriages are seen as pillars of society, highly respected by their peers, family and friends, because that's the facade they present on the surface and no one, including their wives, knows of these clandestine interludes. When wives do become aware (and often this isn't until they think he's having an affair with a woman) they dare not talk about it for fear of being ridiculed or disbelieved. However, when my investigators are out on surveillance on a case involving infidelity, they never take for granted that the third party involved is female.

There are many more bizarre practices we encounter that are too disturbing to document in this book, yet it all goes to prove that you can't tell a person's sexual preferences by his or her appearance, nor should you assume that someone is a saint just because of their standing in the community.

So, as you will already have picked up, my experience isn't based in theory, as is the case with some psychologists, but from years of practical experience of seeing how it really is and not how someone tells you it might be. I'm there when the doubt is nothing more than a feeling. I'm there from the discovery of deception and beyond.

When we talk about deception and betrayal it goes without saying we have to talk about pain, and the element that causes the most pain is lying. When someone you love deceives you by lying, the one thing you can't lose sight of is that your lover has made a conscious choice to deceive you and therefore, to hurt you. What makes lying so disturbing is that no matter how hard you may try to rationalize your lover's behavior (and, believe me, we are all guilty of that—it's the most natural thing in the world to do), lying just doesn't make sense. Why would the one person you love and who tells you he loves you deliberately set out to deceive you? Lying takes away your ability to know what's real anymore. You may find it hard not only to believe what he says or does any longer but also to believe in yourself.

Then we have to deal with the different types of lies— Blatant denials of the truth, and lying by omission. Blatant denials often go something like this: "There's no way I'm having an affair," "I would never do anything to hurt you" and "I'd leave before I did anything like that."

Lying by omission is where the lies are hard to define because they are unspoken. They always involve neglecting to tell you important information that would otherwise affect how you would deal with a particular situation. It's a bit like, "What you don't know won't hurt you." For example, your partner may neglect to tell you he has an anger problem or a drug, alcohol or serious financial problem. Being aware of any of these problems would allow you to choose whether you would want a relationship with this person. Lying by omission doesn't allow you that choice.

Please remember that although I refer to women as the recipients of betrayal, not all men are betrayers and not all betrayers are men. In fact, 50 percent of all betrayers are women; they're just better at it and generally, because they have a plan, they don't get caught as often.

My wish is for you to read this book and walk away with a whole new belief system in place for yourself. I want you to live your life authentically. I want you to expect to be treated with dignity and respect. But most of all I want you to stop doing the same thing day in and day out while expecting different results, because that just won't happen. The bottom line is that for every action there is a reaction. Our thoughts and feelings are motivated by our intentions, and if the intention is to deceive we have to take responsibility for the outcome— there's no other way around it. We can't change other people;

we're only responsible for ourselves, therefore we can only change ourselves, and change we must in order to live a better life.

As women we have been culturally conditioned to be the nurturers, the caregivers and the fix-it people in relationships. I'm very serious when I say that we really do have to wise up and get with the program. The reason we suffer the way we do in situations such as betrayal is so simple—we allow ourselves to be treated this way. We allow it to happen, and as is so often the case, we allow it to continue. Basically we send a message to our partners that says it's OK to treat us this way. Yelling and screaming, ranting and raving or staying silent will do nothing in the long term unless you change your behavior. You set your relationship up how you want it to be.

So here we are in the twenty-first century. Well, that's what I have to keep reminding myself anyway. You would, too, if you worked in my office for a week. I listen to literally thousands of stories about sex, lies and betrayal and not one person is any better equipped than the next in dealing with it. And, you know what, I'm not surprised, but what does surprise me is that we think we should be. Back in the old days, before disposable diapers, when a woman had a baby she had to be shown how to fold and put on a cloth diaper; there wasn't some primal instinct that kicked in, there was a nurse. The same goes for relationships. I suppose our earliest introduction to, and memories of, relationships come from our parents, and that in itself is a scary thought, although it's not their fault. How could our mothers teach us (or their mothers teach them) if *they* didn't know how to maintain a relationship with their husbands without, in many cases, sacrificing a relationship with themselves? Back then mothers didn't teach their daughters how to be feminine, independent, assertive and powerful because they didn't know they could be all of those things. Instead they taught them to be nurturers and homemakers rather than the protectors and providers many women are today.

In my mother's day most women were full-time mothers and took pride in that role. Most women with children today don't have that luxury as they are juggling motherhood and a career and trying to maintain a successful relationship. All of these responsibilities require skills our mothers never had to use. They couldn't teach us what they didn't know.

You might have been lucky enough in high school to have received some sex education. However, sex education is a very different beast to relationship education. What sex education doesn't do is teach you what to look for in a mate, how to relate on an intimate and emotional level and, more importantly, how to be a good partner. If we had never been taught to read and write, how would we know what to do? Of course the answer is that we would be illiterate, and you could say many of us are still illiterate in the relationship sense.

What we must do is learn how to communicate on an intimate and emotional level, but how can we when, even today, as a society we are still embarrassed to talk about sex and intimacy? This never ceases to amaze me—we all got here by the act of sex. If we can do it, why can't we discuss it?

Back in my office I listen to couples who don't know how to communicate what they truly want, feel or need out of fear that their partner won't understand, won't listen or won't care. So many of them lie, cheat and deceive because they figure it's easier. Is it any wonder that many of us at some stage of our lives find ourselves in a mess?

I'm afraid the news isn't very encouraging when we go looking for help from the professionals. Textbook theories might work in a perfect world, but we are far from that. Research tells us that two-thirds of couples attending relationship counseling will be worse off, or no better off, a year down the road. So, if theorizing isn't the answer, what needs to be done?

In reading many books written by psychologists I'm struck by the fact that they always give examples of affairs where the betrayer has admitted his guilt. In all the thousands of clients I've dealt with, I can't remember one example of a husband volunteering that information. Even in the face of irrefutable evidence many will continue to deny their guilt until the evidence is so overwhelming it becomes impossible to keep up the deception. In some cases they never stop denying, no matter how much evidence is thrown at them. In most instances these betrayers have deceived their partner more than once. So that's where textbook psychologists and I part ways and that is why this book had to be written—thousands of women out there suffering at the hands of serial deceivers need help.

When my clients read a book in which the betrayer volunteers his confession and shows his remorse, they can't relate to it. In fact, they feel more disillusioned. They think that there must be something terribly wrong with them for their husbands not to do the same thing. So my way is to lay it out there, warts and all, dispel the myths surrounding infidelity and give good, honest, practical advice on how it really is, not how we think it is.

Often our success in life is defined by how successful our relationships are. Take the couple who has been married for 37 years—they must be successful, right? Not necessarily. Many of my clients are in long-standing marriages but have often suffered more than one betrayal. The marriage only seems good from the outside looking in. Take the person who's been married more than once—like myself. Surely there must be something wrong with me, right? Wrong. Let me tell you something I know for sure: It's a darn sight harder to stay in a destructive relationship living with doubt and stress on a daily basis than it is to leave. It all comes down to what you think you're worth, and having the courage and strength to stand up for yourself in an abusive marriage shows that you respect yourself. I've lost count of the number of marriages of over 30 years' duration in which the woman has stayed in an abusive relationship and has lost all self-respect. And remember, not all abuse is physical; it can also be through control or betrayal.

This book is all about you and looking after you. I'm not interested in anyone else. I'm not going to spend time trying to fix the men in your life. That isn't my intention and it shouldn't be yours. You're not responsible for them. You're only responsible for yourself—and it's you who matters.

This book is meant for people of all ages; after all, you can experience infidelity at any age. While you can't have a full understanding of infidelity unless you have experienced it, to have some understanding of the subject and to be forewarned is better than being totally ignorant about it, as most of us are. My hope is that you will gain sufficient knowledge to alert you to the potential for emotional and financial heartache.

This book should help you understand what I absolutely know. You may be uncomfortable reading some of the chapters (for example, the chapter on how to have an affair), but don't worry too much because I'm going to explode the myth of the perfect affair, which doesn't exist. I'll show you how to spot a cheater from 1000 yards, what you need to know to move through betrayal if you're right in the thick of it, and how to prevent it from happening again.

Finally, there have been a few times during the writing of this book when I've stopped and thought I've been too tough and should have taken a softer approach. And yet the truth is, the reason so many of us have found ourselves dealing with infidelity or betrayal is because the soft approach hasn't worked. When you consider that the vast majority of my clients are between 30 and 60 years of age, there is no excuse for their not knowing right from wrong, or a healthy choice from a destructive one. More often than not the solution lies with the person on the receiving end of infidelity and not the perpetrator. So, if you find this book hard-going at times, I'm not going to apologize. As we know, the truth often hurts, and this book has been written with the very best of intentions. Once you read this book I hope and trust that you will never need to read another book on infidelity.

# one

# DISPELLING THE MYTHS OF INFIDELITY

Have you ever listened to the conversation at a dinner party when the subject comes up of someone you know having an affair? Speculation is rife as to why it's happened and may even contain such gems as: "Poor old Bill's probably not getting it at home so what's he supposed to do?" or "Oh, he's probably just having a midlife crisis," or "It's no big deal, all guys play around," or even "It's probably that new girl he hired; he told me she was hot. She probably came on to him—it's not his fault."

All these comments are purely speculative and based on a number of myths that surround the subject of infidelity. Let me explain how infidelity really works.

If you can smell smoke you can bet there's been a fire. How often have you been to the mailbox to collect the mail without giving it a second thought? Every day? Then one day there's an envelope addressed to you and you don't recognize the handwriting. In your haste to see who sent it, you quickly scan the letter and find it's unsigned. As you start to read the neatly written words, your heart begins to pound and you find yourself frozen to the spot. What you read is numbing and you actually have difficulty registering the words, so you re-read the letter, wondering who could do such a dreadful thing. Who could send a letter saying your husband is having an affair and they thought you should know about it? What type of vindictive, hurtful person could write such words? By now your mind is racing. You look at the writing again; you study the envelope and all the time you're thinking, "This is wrong, why is it addressed to me?"

I'll tell you why it's addressed to you. It's because it's meant for you. Think about it. How often do your happily married friends get letters like this? Never, I bet. This letter is the result of a carefully constructed plan. Usually these carefully constructed plans are masterminded by either a jilted lover or a lover who is trying to bring the relationship to a head, a jealous work colleague or someone who has simply had enough of living with the knowledge that your husband is getting it on with someone behind your back.

In the greater scheme of things, and you won't realize this while your heart is pounding in your ears, this person has actually done you a favor. What was hidden from you may have remained hidden for much longer had it not been brought into the open like this.

I think I have to say at this point that if something like this should ever happen to you and you can honestly say on the deepest intuitive level that you have never had any previous concerns, then, maybe, just maybe, it's come to the wrong address. But if there's one tiny doubt in your mind then it has most likely come to the right address.

Take Claire, for example. When she called me she was hardly able to speak, but after a few attempts through the tears she finally told me that a magazine (you know the kind) had come through the mail addressed to her, and on her twenty-second wedding anniversary, of all days. The sender had written captions on post-it notes and placed them next to certain photos. The captions read: "Your husband likes to do this to me."

As the conversation continued, Claire said that if she were honest there were many times throughout her marriage when Barry's behavior would change and he would become vague and elusive about times and events. Like so many women with a busy lifestyle and family commitments it was easier for Claire to ignore many of the signs.

> I knew Barry was lying when he had these memory lapses and couldn't remember who he had lunch with or what hotel he'd stayed at. He was a lousy liar but I could never prove it. For a time I even convinced myself that Barry was suffering from some kind of dementia. I just needed to believe that the man I had shared 22 years of my life with and two children wasn't a lying cheat because there was always a story, always an answer. Even when the pieces came together and I had seen things with my own eyes, I still doubted myself. Like the time he told me he was going to work over the weekend; I drove to his work and all through the parking lot, both front and back—and his car wasn't there. Then I called his direct line and it rang and went to voicemail, so I tried his cell phone but that was turned off. When Barry finally came home complaining he'd had a hell of a day I told him I had stopped by with lunch but his car wasn't there. He looked at me and said, "What do you mean my car wasn't there? You couldn't have looked very hard—I've been there all day." That was his story

and he was sticking to it. If I continued to challenge him I'd only get the guilt trip: how hard he worked for the kids and me, how lucky I was to have such a great lifestyle. I pretty much knew the drill and could recite it word for word, yet I felt sick to my stomach as I looked at the magazine in my hand and couldn't imagine who would send this to me. What does this woman have that I don't?

Actually, this magazine was meant for Barry. The person who sent it knew the only way to get to him was through Claire.

Let's look at Claire's story in order to dispel some of the myths of infidelity.

## MYTH 1

*"The other woman must be prettier than me."*

Claire couldn't imagine who would do such a thing nor could she imagine what kind of woman had enticed her husband away—was she beautiful, slim, young and sexy? It's a question that has been asked of me thousands of times and the answer is surprisingly difficult for my clients to accept. From time to time your husband might make comments about some luscious creature he's seen on TV and you imagine he wouldn't say no, given half the chance. But in reality the chances are that the luscious creature wouldn't be in the slightest bit interested in him. This is what many women find hard to believe.

My clients are forever telling me how good-looking their husbands are. In other words, they truly believe other women are going to find them irresistible as well, but I have yet to find one of my clients' husbands appealing, and I have literally seen hundreds of photographs of men of all shapes, sizes and ages.

What women have to realize is that men are looking for something quite different. Remember, your husband isn't looking for a wife (he's already got one), he's looking for sex, and I'm afraid to say that the package doesn't have to be that flashy. In essence, it just has to be easy and available. Married men who play are the easiest prey to snare and that's the absolute truth.

And to answer Claire's question—"What is she like?"—the answer is she's a flat-chested, 5-foot-2-inch, mousy brown–haired, size-14 insurance clerk. On the other hand Claire is a 5-foot-8-inch vivacious, attractive, size-6, 40-something financial planning consultant.

In 9 out of 10 cases this is exactly how it is—the "other woman" isn't younger, prettier, slimmer and smarter than you; she's just ready, willing and available.

## MYTH 2

*"He's having a midlife crisis."*

This is clearly illustrated in what Sarah said to me:

> You can't tell me that any man in his right mind is
> going to walk out on a 37-year marriage on Christmas
> Day when his daughter is flying in from England tomor-
> row. Is he having some sort of midlife crisis?

I'm always skeptical when I hear the words "midlife crisis" because I have clients with husbands whose ages range from 20–80, so I'm not sure where "midlife" starts. In Sarah's case, as we delved deeper into her 37-year marriage, it became clear that she had proof of Greg's numerous infidelities, dating back to the earliest years of their marriage. However, this was the first time he'd left her and she felt she needed to give his behavior a label—"midlife crisis." She could use this label to explain to the world the commonly held belief that men of a certain age are prone to infidelity, when in fact her husband had always behaved this way.

What women in Sarah's position need to be aware of is that what Greg did in leaving isn't particularly uncommon for a man in his sixties. His children were all married and living overseas. He and Sarah were very well off financially and he held considerable power in the business world, so in his eyes he'd done his duty by his family. In his head he'd left the marriage many years ago. Sarah, for her part, and like many women, had deeply ingrained beliefs about relationships, handed down through the centuries. Whenever trouble arose Sarah reacted as the nurturer and caregiver, doing everything in her power to right the wrongs, and sending a very clear message to her husband that she would always be there, fixing things when they went wrong.

In behaving this way women set the ground rules for the marriage. Sarah was shocked when Greg left, although his behavior showed he was a prime candidate for this.

The key point here is that you set your relationship up the way you wanted it to be, so you can't ask, "Why has this happened to me?" You have to take responsibility for your part. Greg very clearly showed Sarah that he was a philanderer and a serial philanderer at that, but we all have choices and with those choices comes an element of risk. Sarah's choice was to stay in her marriage.

So, to answer Sarah's question, "No, it's not a midlife crisis—it's a crisis that's been waiting to happen."

## MYTH 3

*"He's not getting it at home."*

It is often assumed that when a man embarks on an affair it is because his wife isn't coming up with the goods. Well, have I got news for you!

This is the story of three attractive, intelligent women: Beverley, Marie and Sue. They all came to me with the same problem—they were living in sexless marriages. Collectively the total amount of celibate time was 43 years and it wasn't for want of trying on their part, contrary to what most people might think.

Combined, their marriages equated to 82 years. Looking at it one way, they had been without sex for almost half their married lives. I know it's hard to imagine anyone would stay in relationships like this but I find this situation to be increasingly common.

Beverley is married to Tom, the managing director of a large and successful company.

> Tom moved out of our matrimonial bed because he said he didn't want to disturb me when he came home late from work functions—and that was 14 years ago ... I always thought it was a weak excuse because I have always been a heavy sleeper.

Marie is married to Frank, a lawyer.

> Frank moved out of our bed, citing that I disrupted his sleep with all my tossing and turning—and that was 16 years ago. What I found strange was that once Frank was in bed he was so exhausted he fell asleep instantly and it would have taken an earthquake registering a ten on the Richter scale to wake him.

Sue is married to Trevor, who owns a large dental practice.

> Trevor told me he felt guilty because he couldn't get an erection so he thought it best to move into the spare room in the hope that loneliness might make something grow harder—that was 13 years ago and according to Trevor it never did.

In Beverley's case we discovered the reason Tom was staying out so late wasn't because of long business meetings or work-related functions but because he'd discovered a lust for very young women and spent his time in massage parlors.

No one could have kept Frank awake, not even the restless Marie, because he was actually living dual lives. He was in a full-blown relationship with a co-worker with whom he had created another home.

Trevor didn't have erectile problems until a few years ago, but then he discovered Viagra. When Sue found four packs of Viagra in his car, the game was up and Trevor was found to have been visiting a family friend every morning on his way to work.

Sex isn't everything in a marriage, but if you talk to the person who isn't getting any, then you realize how important it is. The intimacy you get from a physical relationship is what sets it apart from a friendship. If you have a good physical relationship in your marriage it only rates 15 percent on the scale of importance, but if there's no sex in the relationship it rates 95 percent on the scale of importance. That focus of importance can only have a negative impact on the relationship.

I cannot stress this enough and I'm going to keep on saying it until you get it—you set your relationship up the way you want it to be.

All three of these women have been clients of mine for a long time and all three have received absolute proof of their husband's infidelity. Yet all three have stayed in lonely, sexless marriages, trying at every opportunity to rekindle the fire, while all the time their husbands have been lying and deceiving them. The way in which each has set up their marriage isn't based on a single event or a single action. Not only does each of these women have a dysfunctional relationship with their husband but with themselves as well. These relationships can only exist if they are nurtured and actively encouraged by a lifestyle that supports them. Each one of these women has, through their actions in condoning their husband's behavior, helped shape the lives they are living right now. In fact, the way in which they have set up their marriages and chosen to react to their husband's inappropriate behavior could only have had one result.

At this point let me make myself perfectly clear because I can hear you all screaming, "Condone it? You've got to be kidding!" No doubt some of you will have said something to your husband or partner along the lines of "You do this one more time and it's over, you're out of here. How can you keep doing this to me? I'm going to tell your boss, your mother, your friends and your little floozy that you're a lying, cheating bastard." Yeah, yeah, yeah—he's heard it all before and what do you keep doing? You cook his meals, you wash his clothes, you tidy the house and you keep the home fires burning. You've set your relationship up so that your man has the best of both worlds. Why should he change?

Do you see what I'm saying? Do you get it now? However, the next time you hear the old myth that someone is having an affair because he's not getting it at home, think of Beverley, Marie and Sue, and don't assume it's because the woman doesn't want it.

## MYTH 4

*"Men play around more than women."*

The woman who epitomizes the betraying female has got to be a client of mine named Rose—"Darling, I need you to follow my husband Nigel for a week from 8:30–5:30 and I've got all the information you need. Now, how much do I make the check out for?"

We did as she asked and followed him for seven days. He never put a foot wrong. It got to the point where we were sure we had missed something. The only odd thing that happened was on the fifth day of surveillance when he decided to go home in the middle of the afternoon and we reported to Rose that he was on his way. There was a change in her voice and she sounded as though she was out of breath, but nothing was said and we continued as we had done for the previous week.

After reporting back to Rose on one of the most uneventful weeks of surveillance on record, she seemed very happy. This is why:

> Ten years ago Nigel had an affair with one of my closest friends and the very foundations of my life were shattered. But I wasn't about to let the man whom I had supported through medical school ride roughshod over me. As for my friend, I slowly distanced myself from her to the point where we haven't spoken for eight years. Neither of them has any idea that I know what happened and they never will.
>
> So from that moment on I devised a plan, which would ensure that Nigel continued to rise to the top of the medical profession, allowing me to do all the things I had wanted to do but had forsaken in order to put him where he is today. Nigel had no interest in taking vacations, so I began to travel and in particular to pursue a love of skiing. On a visit to Aspen I met David, a young (20 years younger than me) lawyer and we became lovers. We traveled to many different destinations until one day I decided that my plan would be unfinished until I had brought him to New Zealand. And so to ensure I wasn't caught with my panties off I employed you and your team to watch poor, unsuspecting Nigel and that is what he is still today. Isn't life great?

So you can see that women seek revenge in a very underhanded way. Women often leave articles of clothing or jewelry in their lover's house or car, especially if he's been promising to leave his wife. They think this might help the process along but in general it rarely helps the situation and there are no winners.

However, when it comes to the woman scorned then look out—revenge is sweet and you had better believe it. Rose gets a buzz from continuing to exact her revenge and because of her skillful manipulation, planning and ability to make opportunities out of her difficulties, to this day Nigel remains oblivious.

Jeff's wife Kate is very typical of the female mindset in that if she thinks she can bring her love interest into the home, then make no mistake, that is exactly what she will do—with you there. The difference is that men will take their lovers home but nine times out of ten you won't be there.

> If I told you that when my wife goes swimming at the local pool and she returns home with her swimsuit and towel wet but they don't smell of chlorine, what would you think? She's not the type to have an affair.

Let's answer Jeff's question logically. The pool she swims at is chlorinated and since Kate's swimsuit and towel don't smell of chlorine she hasn't been swimming there. Jeff's following statement is very common among men: "Kate's not the type to have an affair." Well, what type of woman is she and what type is it that has affairs?

I'll let Jeff explain the rest.

> My wife Kate is a keen swimmer but to be honest I've never enjoyed the water but always wanted our children to learn, so when Kate started to take the children to evening classes ... I was happy for her to indulge her love of the water while teaching the kids to swim. After a few weeks Kate began to talk about a guy she'd met

named Colin who also took his children to the pool and how he and his wife Jill, who often picked them up, seemed like a nice couple and perhaps we should invite them over for a barbecue one Sunday.

It seemed like a good idea and we all got along well, with the kids having a great time. Slowly, Colin and Jill became a fixture in our lives and joined our circle of friends, and six months later we all went on vacation together. The only thing we didn't have in common with our respective spouses was swimming, as both Jill and I hated it, so Kate and Colin would take the kids to the water at every opportunity. Then about 18 months ago Kate and Colin decided they needed more competition and so in addition to the Tuesday-night swim sessions with the kids they started training together for triathlons, which meant Thursday training at the local pool and Sunday morning cycling and running. We continued to socialize and spend considerable time together until one night Kate returned from one of those Thursday-night training swims, and, as she undressed and emptied her sports bag, the one thing missing was the unmistakable smell of chlorine. I said nothing at the time but each Thursday after training I waited for that most unmistakable of smells but never did it enter my senses again.

We found the reason for a lack of chlorine was that when we followed Kate she went to a hotel across town where she was greeted by the reception staff like a long-standing customer. She paid the bill in cash and went to her room and within five minutes a taxi with Colin in the back drew up and he went straight up in the elevator to join her. Further inquires showed she had booked the room in her maiden name and the reason for her being so well known was because she'd booked that same room for the last 18 months and it was booked on the same night for the next 12 months.

Kate did what a lot of women do. Women are drawn by a strong emotional connection as well as a strong physical connection. This was shown by the fact that Kate brought Colin and Jill into their circle of friends in order to spend more time with Colin than would have been possible under the circumstances of a normal affair. Through her planning, Kate and Colin managed to deceive their partners by using friendship and children as a cover. When women like Kate are finally uncovered, their downfall doesn't come from their husband's intuition, because Jeff had been oblivious to the ongoing emotional deception and certainly hadn't noticed a change in her behavior. What he had noticed was a physical change in terms of a lack of chlorine smell.

So, in trying to dispel the myth that men play around more than women, you must understand how this conclusion was reached. You only have to switch on the news or open a newspaper and there it is—another rich, famous and powerful man is having an affair. How often do you see a woman of similar standing shown in this position? Very rarely, I would say. With the exception of the late Princess Diana I can't think of any. Throughout history how many powerful women (and there have been many) have been shown to be adulterers? And yet throughout history from Henry VIII to John F. Kennedy and now Bill Clinton, rich, famous and powerful men have often been shown to have marital affairs. These have been condoned or somewhat trivialized or even depicted as their birthright. Women on the other hand are castigated and called harlots, whores and sluts, and in many countries are put to death for those same marital infidelities.

In modern Western society there are just as many women betraying as men and the reason we don't hear or read about it is that women plan their infidelities and men don't. Generally women deal with love, sex, friendship and partner-

ship on a very different level than men. This doesn't mean
their needs are any different and that is where men make the
mistake—in assuming their wives wouldn't play around.
Women use this way of thinking to their advantage.

A second advantage for the woman who wants to play is
that men are less intuitive by a country mile and just don't pick
up on the small things. This, in combination with a good dol-
lop of male arrogance (9 out of 10 men when asked if they
thought their wives would cheat on them said no), gives plenty
of scope for a woman to carry on an extramarital affair with
little chance of being found out.

My experiences show that women plan for the possibility of being caught and men don't, or more importantly don't
care. When I have posed the question to men, "Did you ever
consider you might get caught?" the usual reply has been, "No,
I'll deal with it if it happens."

I don't want to appear unsympathetic but this book is all
about reality and in many cases men are the masters of their
own demise. Just as women who stay with their philandering
husbands out send a message that says it's OK to be treated
this way, men also need to be aware of what's happening
around them and be conscious of the little things. By appearing uninterested you only make it easier for the woman with
betrayal on her mind to carry it through.

## MYTH 5

*"There's got to be something wrong with her or he
wouldn't stray."*

In Myth 1 it is the wife asking the question of the other
woman ("Is she younger, sexier, etc.?"), whereas in this myth
it is the wife who is under question. However, on the surface
of this myth is the perception that the betrayed is imperfect or

lacking in some way, such as being less attractive, less intelligent, dowdy or dull when in reality it isn't true. In reality it has nothing to do with the woman and everything to do with the man who is cheating. To prove this you only have to look at the late Princess Diana, Jerry Hall, Liz Hurley, Nicole Kidman and Halle Berry. These women have been recognized as some of the world's most beautiful and desirable and yet their men, who would be hard-pressed to find anyone of equal caliber, and who you would therefore think would be more than content with them, have still betrayed them.

So, you tell me what's wrong with these women that they have been betrayed? These are all beautiful, intelligent, vivacious and talented women. What other qualities could they possibly possess to prevent this from happening to them? Can you see the picture emerging that it isn't the betrayed with the problem but the betrayer?

What I find interesting in my work is that 95 percent of my clients are attractive, intelligent professional women but they never thought they would be betrayed. They thought, like the rest of you, that it only happened to the dull and dowdy. The reason it hits so hard is partly because they are intelligent and can't believe they chose a philanderer as a partner because they thought they were smarter than that. Because they do take pride in how they look and present themselves, the biggest blow comes when they eventually find that their husband's love interest is as I described in Myth 1—someone who isn't as attractive, who isn't smarter and who isn't even younger than them.

A good example of what a man is prepared to risk all for is Hugh Grant with Divine Brown. Grant was certainly not looking for a relationship; he hadn't fallen in love with someone else and Divine Brown sure as hell couldn't hold a candle to Liz Hurley when it came to the looks department. However, that moment struck the death knell for their relationship.

An example from my files is a client named Debbie. She's typical of my clients in that she is an attractive, intelligent career woman in her early forties. Due to business commitments Debbie travels abroad one week in each month.

> I'm sure my husband is up to something. He's been acting strangely of late and every time I come home from overseas he seems really uptight. God, this is so hard and I hope you tell me I'm wrong, but I've got this feeling and it won't go away. On my last trip I came home unexpectedly and found his scrunched-up cell phone bill in the kitchen trash, and when I examined it there was this one number that jumped out at me because he had called it six times a day, every day, for the time I was away. So I called it and I think I recognized the voice but I can't be sure. It sounded like the woman he used to go out with before me. I've seen her and she is absolutely ghastly and I would never have thought she was his type ... I'm probably wrong because I'm sure Steve told me that she'd just gotten married recently. Anyway I guess what I'm wanting is to have him watched the next time I'm away.

Steve had gone to play golf and we could see him on the veranda of the clubhouse with his playing partners. His car was at the rear of the parking lot out of sight of the clubhouse, and as we watched a battered old BMW pulled into a space next to his car. Within minutes Steve appeared, pulling his golf cart and bag and began loading his car. He then went to the passenger window of the BMW and leaned in. He then got back into his own car, and both vehicles left the parking lot. They drove to a nearby reserve, where she got out of her car and into his. The first thing we noticed was that there was no sign of a wedding ring. Now it takes a lot to shock me but shocked I was because this woman, apart from her height and hair coloring, was the complete opposite of Debbie. Her hair didn't look as though it had been washed for days and she looked as though she had been poured into her clothes—they were so tight there was bulging flesh everywhere, but judging by their actions Steve didn't seem to mind at all. Now Steve is what you might call affluent and so the second surprise was when they dined at Burger King, which led me to think that Steve didn't have to blow the budget on this woman.

## MYTH 6

*"He would never bring anyone into the matrimonial home."*

There are two forms of this insidious behavior and both are extremely common. The first form is where the act of infidelity is taking place outside of the matrimonial home but the husband or wife finds ways in which to introduce their betraying partner either into their circle of friends or have them invited to parties and social functions.

When Celine finally confronted Josh about his affair with his work colleague Georgina, she was shocked when she realized how many times Georgina had been to her home for barbecues and dinner parties over the previous two years. Then there had been so many company functions Josh had organized and Georgina had more often than not attended on her own since her partner, according to Josh, was always away on business.

Only after the evidence became irrefutable did Josh finally admit that the stolen moments during the week with Georgina hadn't been enough, and so the only way in which they could see each other more often was to invite Georgina into his home with the cover of her partner. This offered a false sense of security to Celine.

The second and most blatant form of this behavior is when the betrayer takes his lover back to the matrimonial bed. This is the hardest thing for any woman to accept because not only are they themselves not considering infidelity, but the house is their home and the last place they would want to defile. The first thing a woman should do is to stop thinking along their own moral lines and consider that if he's having an affair then he isn't playing by any rules but his own and that means anything is possible—including sex with another woman in the matrimonial bed.

There are a number of reasons for men taking their lovers home. Some men will avoid spending a dollar if they have to and there is no paper trail to worry about, unlike a hotel or illicit weekend away. For some men there is the perverse excitement of snubbing their nose at their wife by having sex in the home.

I went away on business for three days and came home earlier than expected. Although the house was empty it looked as though Des hadn't been out since I left. The place was a mess and when I went into the bedroom I noticed the bed was unmade and there was a pile of crumpled tissues on the bedside table. When I picked them up a used condom fell to the floor. As I bent down to pick the condom up Des walked in and when he noticed me dangling the spent condom in my hand, his expression resembled that of a stunned fish. I asked him to explain and he said he'd masturbated that morning, to which I replied, "Since when have you become a hygiene freak? Did you not want your hand to catch anything?" There was no answer and in my eyes there was no other explanation; Des had committed the greatest sin of all, shitting in his own nest.

## MYTH 7

*"She's just someone he can talk to but it's not sexual."*

For a client to call me, their intuition is telling them that although this is what he is saying they can't quite accept it's true. They try to rationalize by starting the conversation with these words—it's their way of justifying and minimizing the facts. It's like when people use the expression, "I slept with so and so," when in actual fact they are having sex with that person but the word "sleeping" makes it all sound more acceptable.

Let's be honest here—the words aren't coming from the client but from their partner. This is what he has said to her and he is doing exactly what she is doing when she is talking to me—minimizing and justifying.

In all my experience of clients using these words or similar, the true fact of the matter is that the betrayers never get to eat, drink or sleep together because they're too busy stealing moments during the day to have sex.

Emma was out shopping and saw her husband sitting at an outside café table with a young woman she recognized from his work.

> I watched them for about 15 minutes and their conversation was quite animated as they leaned in to one another across the table. When Justin came home I waited for him to raise the subject but he spoke about everything else except his coffee with the woman from work. I became agitated and in the end said that a friend of mine had seen him having coffee with a woman and

why hadn't he told me about it when he had discussed everything else about his day. At first he said he'd forgotten and then changed his mind saying it was unimportant but she was getting married soon and they'd been discussing her wedding plans over coffee. This had me boiling for a number of reasons, firstly because this café was miles from their office but more importantly because when we decided to marry, Justin left all the planning to me and all he had to do was turn up and then he couldn't even get that right because he was late. So I said to him, "Since when have you been employed as a wedding planner?" but instead of an answer he just said they found each other easy to talk to and "Hey, nothing's going on if that's what you're getting at." At that point he stormed out and I was left to sit and consider what I had seen and his reaction to my questions. Over the next few days I thought I'd managed to justify everything to myself but my intuition was saying the opposite, so I picked up the phone and discovered there was no wedding because there was no fiancé, no boyfriend, no man in sight but my husband, her lover.

## MYTH 8

*"Where does he find the time to fit infidelity into his busy day?"*

Again there is an assumption here that infidelity, betrayal, call it what you like, is about love, romance and intimacy when in fact it's about sex—plain and simple. So when this question is asked, think about how long it takes to have a sandwich and coffee and then consider the time from penetration to ejaculation. A quick interlude is hardly a grand romance and getting to know you and meeting family and friends doesn't come into the picture, so an hour would be a luxury and 15 minutes is fine and plenty of time to get the deed done.

Remember: motels offer daily and hourly rates; parks and reserves are free; cars are cramped but mobile; boats are private and secluded and there is always home. Most married people when playing with another married person have to choose these snatched moments during the day to avoid alerting their spouses, so don't be surprised if they're home in the evening because the deed is being done by day.

Another form of betrayal is the variety that you pay for, where she supplies the room and all the necessities to have some fun. Times can vary from 15 minutes to an hour and can be booked ahead of time or just taken on the spot.

Some time ago when I was watching a client's husband, who was suspected of having an affair, I parked across the road from his office outside a beauty therapist's establishment. There was a sandwich board outside on the street offering facials, manicures, therapeutic massage and, down at the very bottom, stress relief. I must have sat there for most of the morning before I realized I hadn't seen one woman go in or out of this establishment. However, over lunchtime I noticed trade became quite brisk with men wearing everything from business suits to shorts entering and leaving the premises. Then I noticed my client's husband enter; he re-emerged an hour later looking extremely relaxed and relieved of stress. He then went on, bought a sandwich and went back to work.

During that time I decided to time the men coming in and out and found they were spending between 15 minutes to an hour inside. So to confirm my suspicions I sent one of my male investigators in to inquire about their services. He was told 15 minutes for a handjob, 30 minutes for oral sex and an hour for full intercourse. So while my client thought her husband was munching away on a chicken sandwich he was actually … I'll leave it up to your imagination.

## MYTH 9

*"It wasn't his fault—she threw herself at him and seduced him."*

In Myth 7 (she's just someone he can talk to but it's not sexual) I said that my client's intuition is telling them that although this is what he is saying they can't quite accept it's true. Again in this myth the words are there to mislead you into rationalizing, justifying and minimizing the facts.

Take Grant, for example, who, after being caught, went into great detail explaining to his wife how he wasn't even attracted to the woman he'd just had sex with. When she tried to justify his actions to me I pointed out in my usual diplomatic manner that if she was prepared to believe this garbage then there was little point in trying to convince her otherwise. However, she decided to listen as I explained the facts as they really are. To get an erection there has to be some sort of attraction, and so I asked her were they both fully clothed when sex took place. To which she replied, "Well, no, he told me they were naked."

"So what you're saying to me is that their clothes just fell off. Did she have a gun?"

"What do you mean, did she have a gun?"

"Well, firstly he wasn't attracted to her but got an erection and then, having not been attracted to her and got an erection, he took his clothes off, so I have to assume that after all of that and then to have intercourse she must have threatened to shoot him in the balls, because if she didn't, there is no excuse."

In conclusion—the fear of being shot in the balls would make any self-respecting erection disappear at an amazing rate.

The reality is that he was attracted to her, he wanted her and he had her—and that is the only explanation for what he did.

## MYTH 10

*"All men play around, don't they?"*

This question infuriates me because clients use it to justify their partner's behavior. If all men play around, why should they feel bad about it? This statement is a cop-out, which comes from a woman who is too afraid to face the truth; it is easier to accept the devil you know than the devil you don't by convincing yourself that any other man is going to be the same as the one you have. Therefore, what's the point in thinking she could make a difference?

Sometimes when I hear this question I know exactly why it's being asked and what brought it about. The client has irrefutable proof of her husband's infidelity, in fact so much proof he can't do anything but admit to the affair. However, he has immediately put Plan B into effect—minimization. I can hear him now: "Look, I don't know why you're making such a big deal about this. Everyone does it. I'm not unique. I can give you thousands of cases, and anyway it's over now and it won't happen again." Acceptance of this type of behavior is borne out of fear and women who believe this are very wrong indeed.

Of course not all men play around; there are many men of integrity out there and the sooner women realize this the better.

## MYTH 11

*"This will shock you."*

All my clients think their story is unique and that I will be shocked. All cases are different in that the protagonists vary in the degree of emotional entanglement and hurt they feel, but throughout all the thousands of cases I have dealt with, there are common threads and behavioral patterns that link them all. Because infidelity is so devastating to them and they have an emotional connection they expect me to be shocked at their story. However, I would liken it to an undertaker who deals with death daily—when you call him to tell him a relative of yours has died you don't expect him to be shocked. So why should they expect it from me? The reason is that we can talk more freely about death than infidelity or betrayal because infidelity and betrayal is about sex and that is something that most people find difficult to discuss at the best of times. For me (like the undertaker) there are new casualties every day so I have pretty much seen and heard it all.

## MYTH 12

*"Julia, there must be danger in your job."*

Most people assume there must be an element of danger in my work and I suppose to a degree there is, but not the sort you may think. The only danger I face is stress and it goes with the territory. Infidelity is such an emotionally charged topic that there will always be a handful of people you're never going to please no matter what you do. Usually these people are the ones who have allowed a situation to go on for far too long and then want a quick fix. It's incredible how some clients have been seduced out of hundreds of thousands of dollars, have been emotionally betrayed for years, have spent thousands of dollars on lawyers, yet if I don't come up with the goods immediately all their problems become my fault. I had one such client not so long ago and the call went something like this:

> Oh, Julia I can't believe I've been so stupid. How could I have been so blind? Everybody has been telling

me for years that he's been ripping me off, but why would someone do that? What makes a person do such things? I'm such a mess. I don't know what to do. He's left me and I think he's with another woman, but why would he do this to me? He's only just got back from four months overseas and I never questioned him about what he does when he's away. He doesn't even have to work because I do that. I don't think he's having sex with this woman, but I need to know who she is.

An hour or so later I calmed her down enough to tell her she should see her doctor just to get herself something to help her through the initial stages. I don't advocate the taking of drugs but sometimes it's just too overwhelming to handle without help and it certainly was for this woman. I also gave her the name of a relationship law specialist because I felt that was going to be more effective at the stage she was at than my services, considering he had already left and had been fleecing her financially for years. Who the other woman was at this time was immaterial and we could always follow up on that at a later date if she felt the need. She went on to tell me that for the last 20 years she had basically kept this man: bought him cars, paid for overseas trips he would take on his own, and yet she would never question what he was doing and she would have no contact with him at all while he was away.

I know what you're thinking. You're thinking I must be making this up because no one could be that stupid. Well, I'm not, and this is not an isolated case. This woman is a success in business and very intelligent, but emotionally challenged. As the conversation continued I had to start popping vitamins to help keep the stress levels down because this story went from bad to worse.

She had found emails from a number of women he'd met overseas, which spoke of their passion, lust and feelings for this man, and yet she still believed he was being faithful to her despite telling me that the one thing in the world he wanted to be was a porn star!

She said she couldn't go on without finding out who the current woman was and asked if I could find out for her. She had an address where she thought her ex-partner was living. I told her we could and then carried out some surveillance at this property, but lo and behold she turned up wanting to play detective. As far as we are concerned this is an absolute no-go area—you either leave us to do the job or you do it yourself. The last thing my investigators need is some emotionally charged person getting in the way.

No matter what I said she wouldn't listen and one didn't have to be Houdini to work out why this man had behaved like this. He'd had all the opportunity in the world and she had allowed it, but because I hadn't come up with the answers she wanted to hear I was useless. Even if I had she would have wanted more, so I will make a prediction that I wasn't the first investigator she'd called and my commiserations are with the next.

Another frustration is clients who confront their husband or partner with every snippet of information they've obtained during the ongoing surveillance. This alerts him to be careful, which makes our job so much harder and longer and in some cases can completely blow any chance of catching him. There are times when I feel that some clients subconsciously sabotage the investigation because they cannot confront the reality.

If you are going to hire a private investigator, you will need to have thought through exactly what you are going to do with the information and how you are going to deal with the "worst case scenario." I find that this is where clients fall down. They expect to be proven wrong and when the opposite occurs they aren't prepared to deal with it.

## KEY POINTS

- The lover doesn't have to be younger, prettier, sexier or slimmer than you. No, they just have to be up for it and let's face it—there's no easier prey than a married man looking for sex.

- Forget using midlife crisis as an excuse for infidelity because if he's that kind of guy and he's got a pulse, then he's a risk.

- "He's having an affair because he's not getting it at home, right?" Wrong!

- "Men play around more than women." Wrong! Women just don't get caught as often.

- "There's got to be something wrong with her for him to stray." Yeah, right! So tell me what excuse did Tom Cruise have with Nicole Kidman? Mick Jagger with Jerry Hall? Hugh Grant with Elizabeth Hurley? Hell, if something was wrong with these women what chance is there for the rest of us?

- "He would never bring anyone back to the matrimonial home." You want to bet, because when the small head is leading the big head, all reasoning goes out of the window. Men just don't have the same emotional attachment to the family home as women do.

- "She's just someone he can talk to but it's not sexual." Yeah! And pigs can fly.

- "Where does he find the time to fit infidelity into his busy day?" Anytime between 15 and 60 minutes because this is about sex, period!

- "It wasn't his fault she threw herself at him and seduced him." He knows right from wrong and made a conscious decision to betray. Don't fall for the "It just happened" story, because how often do your clothes fall off of their own accord?

- "All men play around, don't they?" No!

43

# SIGNS OF BETRAYAL

## Intuition

How can something you can't even see be so powerful? Maybe you don't realize that in contrast to every other species in nature, we consciously choose to ignore and not even recognize intuitive signals. We disregard our intuition unless we can find a logical explanation for it. Even when our intuitive feelings are strong and clear, so often we seek other options rather than trust ourselves. The amount of emotional energy we use looking for a safe explanation could be put to better use evaluating the information we have. Let me explain how intuition shows itself to you: gut feelings; nagging feelings and thoughts; suspicion; doubt; hunches and apprehension.

So if you've opted to disregard your intuition up to now but the signals are still persistent, then you may just have overlooked the signs of betrayal your intuition is telling you are there.

# The Signs

## LET'S GET PHYSICAL

Out of the blue your man says it's time to lose a bit of weight, tone up the old body and generally get in shape. Any sudden changes in behavior are key signs. For example, Sue's husband hadn't been a slob by any means; he enjoyed his food but apart from a couple of games of golf he did little to keep fit. Then he decided to join a gym, but not one close to home where he and Sue could work out together but on the other side of town and even then some distance from his office. When Sue inquired why he'd joined a gym so far from home he trotted out the excuses that it was cheaper and they ran programs for people who were just starting to get in shape again.

And so his new regimen started but we found out his workout regimen was a little different than the one he'd told Sue about. Yes, he did go to the gym early each morning but on some days and especially on a Saturday (Sunday was his day of rest), he would join his lover at her home—where he would still get extremely physical in the horizontal position.

So what was it that alerted Sue to his indiscretion? Well, first of all it was the obvious, the sudden change in behavior. But second and most important, it was that a gym with such a cheap membership scheme could afford the most expensive French soap for their showers!

## SEX, TOO MUCH OR NOT ENOUGH

When someone withdraws sexually from you or wants more sex or starts suggesting positions you've never used before then again we're looking at sudden changes in behavior.

Sarah and David had been married for 28 years when he began to ask her to try new ways and positions. When Sarah mentioned this, David became defensive and said they'd done these things before and she'd just forgotten. Sarah was sure she would have remembered these acts and positions as they were very different from their normal lovemaking. Of course, this change in behavior alerted her so she began a little detective work of her own. Sifting through his credit card statements Sarah began to find strange companies listed. When she showed these to me I instinctively knew none of them would have listings in the telephone directory since they are fronts for massage parlors—a little surveillance work proved the point.

When the opposite occurs and someone withdraws from you it's important to remember there are different degrees of withdrawal, from a slowing of your normal sexual activity to a complete stop. The slowing down of sexual activity can often show the sign of a lustful or emotional attachment elsewhere and a complete stop is often the sign of a fantasy being fulfilled. Anyone will have difficulty in competing with this. It can also be seen when your partner withdraws to the spare room, citing sleep disturbance as an excuse.

Increased sexual activity brought about by your partner is often to lull you into a false sense of security. This happened to Jackie, who couldn't get over Damien's new zest for making love. When she asked him if he was seeing someone else he told her if he had any more sex he'd be dead. Jackie wasn't put off the scent for long and employed us to check him out, and so it was shown that his actions spoke louder than his words since his sexual activity at home was more than matched by his sexual activity elsewhere.

## BREASTFEEDING THE CELL PHONE

Secrecy is one of the biggest giveaways that someone is betraying you. There's nothing wrong with one's own privacy but excessive secrecy in a marriage is another thing altogether. Watch how someone behaves with his or her cell phone. Do they:

- keep it close to them at all times?
- take it in the bathroom with them?
- take it with them when they take the garbage out?
- constantly look at their phone (a giveaway for text messages)?
- when you are close by and it rings do they start walking away out of earshot?
- leave it in the car or switched off and occasionally check for messages?

The key here is that when you have nothing to hide you hide nothing. When your partner is hiding something from you, you'll notice that the phone bill, bank statements and credit card statements conveniently end up at work, and in fact nothing comes home at all. Recently one of my investigators was picking up the company mail from the post office box and noticed a man also checking his mail. When he opened his cell phone bill he tore up the list of calls made into very small pieces. He then threw these into the trash can, wrote a check for the amount of the bill and dropped this in the mail. Think about it—when you have nothing to hide you hide nothing.

So when you ask to see these records, whether it's for phone or credit card, your requests can cause a huge problem. You may be told they've been thrown away or they'll be brought home but they never seem to materialize. Don't accept these excuses because records are kept for seven years and a simple phone call to the phone or credit card company will elicit them within a few days.

## CELL PHONE BILLS

The cell phone bill is a sure-fire giveaway of someone who is having an affair. The sheer number of calls should be all the proof you need. I say "should be" because in my experience it never is. Don't be swayed by excuses such as: "She's a work colleague. What do you want me to do, send smoke signals?" No matter how hard he tries to talk his way out there is no way out. A cell phone bill is tangible evidence and that is why a cell phone call summary is the first thing that's removed once an affair begins. Getting your hands on a call summary is always a bonus.

Should you manage to find the summary, you may notice a certain phone number has been called eight times in one day, then ten the next and five the next and so on, so you decide to call it and a female answers.

Then you need to look at the times and lengths of the calls and compare them with the times and lengths of calls he makes to you. I'll bet there is a huge discrepancy in favor of the calls made to her.

Now you need to look and see if he calls you right after one of those calls. You may see a pattern emerging—when he calls her then you, it's usually to see what you're up to and to reassure himself everything is fine at home. If his phone is off for any length of time during the day you may see she gets the first call when it's back on, and then you again. This is his way of continually reassuring himself you are oblivious to his deception. As you go through the account you'll see this kind of pattern repeated a number of times. It's easy to figure it out. First ask the obvious, and that is, have you seen this sort of pattern before? Think about this. If you have a platonic male friend, do you call him between five and ten times per day? Do you call him first thing in the morning and last thing at night? Do you make very short calls (leave messages) or text messages on the weekend? Somehow I don't think so because we don't even call our best girlfriends that many times a day.

But if you're in lust, well, that's different, and to hear their voice is the next best thing to seeing them.

Betrayers are switching to the use of prepaid phones to conduct their affairs. This is because there are no phone bills to contend with and so the betrayer feels he has less chance of getting caught. If you've noticed certain numbers being dialed on his normal phone that have now stopped appearing on his bill, this can be a sign of him using a prepaid cell. You need to check credit and debit card statements from around the time that these numbers stopped appearing for purchases from stores or suppliers and for the purchase of prepaid cards, as this is often the way in which these phones are replenished with minutes. Most people buy these prepaid cards in quite large denominations and use a credit card to purchase them. Also check for patterns of cash withdrawals that can't be substantiated by a receipt.

It is likely the prepaid phone will never be seen in your home and will be hidden either at work or in the car. Good places to check are under the driver and passenger seats or, if the car has a fold-down back seat, check under there. The spare tire compartment is also another hiding place, as is the compartment that holds the car jack and tools. If you can gain access to his briefcase then search that, too, although in these circumstances this is likely to be kept locked.

Once again, remember the saying, "If you have nothing to hide you hide nothing."

## RECEIPTS, BANK STATEMENTS AND CREDIT CARD BILLS

Have you ever been really excited by a receipt you found while innocently emptying your husband's pockets? For example, a receipt from a jewelry store for a gold bracelet when it's your birthday in a few days' time? Have you ever had that sinking feeling as your birthday comes and goes with no sign of a gold bracelet? Instead you get a card with the promise of a vacation, only you've had those promises before and the vacations have never materialized. If you ask him to explain what the receipt was all about he jumps down your throat and accuses you of snooping. Then he tells you how you've spoilt the surprise so now you can forget it. A reaction like that is guilt at being caught deceiving you.

I had a client who called me because she found such a receipt, and she was furious, not because her husband had bought some gold earrings, but because she couldn't understand him buying such inexpensive ones she would never wear. She knew full well they weren't meant for her as her husband was very well aware of her very expensive tastes. As you can see, the humble receipt can tell many stories.

The same applies to credit card bills. How many times have you tried to figure out some odd amounts from companies you can find no record of? These aren't usually for huge amounts; often they're for just over $100 and there isn't usually any pattern—unless, of course, you bring them to your husband's attention. Then the only pattern you'll notice is that they never appear again. These companies are the fronts for massage parlors. All massage parlors have confidential credit card facilities so it looks benign on your credit card bill. When you're searching for these amounts look for company names with the word "Holdings" in the title then try doing a company search and you'll find there will be no street address, no phone number listing. In many cases no such company will exist.

Bank statements can be another giveaway, as one client found when she was looking for an amount she had paid for car repairs and discovered a cash withdrawal at the same time each week. She discovered this was child support for a child she knew nothing about but that had been conceived during their marriage.

## TOO MANY DETAILS

When someone wants to deceive you, a technique that is often used is giving too many details. When someone is telling the truth they don't feel the need to go into great detail. For example, if they were late meeting you for lunch they would simply say they were sorry for being late. But someone who is lying needs to justify the lie to themself. Their reasoning probably sounds plausible to you but it doesn't to them so they keep on talking, trying to add additional support to their story. Take, for example, the guy who called his wife and started to describe the plane trip, every turbulent bump, what he'd eaten and who sat next to him. The only problem was that he hadn't taken the plane trip at all and his wife was receiving his call in the same hotel foyer as he was making it from. She told me later that if she hadn't seen him with her own eyes she would have believed his story, although it was a little over the top. He was a regular flyer and normally wouldn't have described such a mundane internal flight.

## GETTING DEFENSIVE

You'll notice when you ask what used to be a simple question, such as "When will you be home?" he becomes defensive, and if you challenge him he can become verbally aggressive. The surfacing of this behavior is usually a sign that guilt is lurking somewhere. His response becomes a verbal assault, such as, "I'm sick of being questioned. I can't do anything right and no matter what I do it's not good enough. You always think I'm doing something. Why don't you call everyone and ask them what I'm doing? I'm trying to do what you want." So now it's turned onto you and you're probably feeling really bad for asking a simple question. Answers like this reek of guilt; the easiest way for a betrayer to camouflage the lies is to turn it around and attack the innocent party.

## OVERLY ATTENTIVE

Remember what I said before? That sudden changes in behavior are tell-tale signs? So, if you've lived with a guy who's never taken much notice of what you wear and what you do, then all of a sudden he starts complimenting you on how you look or decides it's time you had a vacation away from the kids and on your own because you work so hard and deserve the break, beware. Especially if he is displaying any of the other signs we've talked about.

Take Tricia's husband, for example. He did just that. He suggested she needed a break and because things were so busy for him at work she should go on her own to New York for three weeks. That's when she telephoned me because it was so out of character—he'd never been so considerate in their 16 years of marriage. We only had to watch for the first week because he never went home after that and couldn't be contacted by phone at home. Wouldn't you just know it—the phone lines were out for two weeks. Our inquiries showed no faults were found and the phone was off the hook the whole time.

## TALKING ABOUT A PARTICULAR PERSON TOO MUCH

This doesn't mean they have to be positive comments. What we have found is that sometimes a man will come home from work, as Roy did, and start to make derogatory comments about a new female colleague. Roy would tell Natalie how useless the new colleague was at work. He would also throw in comments about how she was no oil painting, knowing full well that in the short term making comments such as these would put Natalie at ease. The problem for Roy came when Natalie began to notice how many times this woman's name was mentioned. When someone is attracted to a person that person is always in their thoughts and to talk about them, even in an unflattering way, is an excuse for the guilty party to keep that person in their mind. When Roy first started behaving this way, Natalie, like so many women, thought nothing of it but she started to notice not a day went by without his mentioning her.

Natalie had to go out of town for a night and had Roy watched. True to form Roy had his little oil painting over to watch some naughty movies.

Another way men try to cover their tracks is by talking about the new female they have met and their husband or boyfriend or the fact that she's soon to be married. All these scenarios are little smokescreens. They think the simple mention of a man in the same breath as a woman will keep the wife off the scent. Peter told Viv that his personal assistant Sally was finally getting married in six months' time and was impossible to work with because she was so preoccupied with her wedding arrangements. Peter even went as far as to invite them over for dinner. However, at the last minute Sally's fiancé wasn't feeling well and couldn't make it. Peter suggested she come anyway. I remember Viv telling me how uncomfortable she felt that night. She said watching the pair of them was like intruding on a private relationship. We later found out there was no fiancé or wedding and that Peter and Sally had been having an affair for 18 months.

## HANG-UP CALLS AND STRANGE
## MESSAGES FROM THE UNKNOWN

I think not! I'm always intrigued as to how women can find logical reasons to justify strange hang-up calls in the middle of the night or cards, letters, magazines and newspaper cuttings that come in the mail. These are all very obvious signs of betrayal and usually come from a dumped lover or in some cases from someone who knows what's going on and wants to alert the wife. However, it is usually from a woman scorned.

The one fundamental thing women who have affairs with married men forget is that the man they're involved with is lying to his wife. Why does the other woman think he's telling her the truth? When she finally realizes that what she thought was the truth is actually a lie (and he's never going to leave his wife), that's when the chances are heightened that such unexplained mail or calls from an anonymous person may reach you.

The husband of one of my clients got in first. He knew there was a very real possibility that something along these lines could happen, so he told his wife a crazed woman was stalking him. The only thing that didn't stack up was that he never reported this alleged stalking to the police. Of course, the reason he didn't report it was obvious; the woman in question was far from crazed and the only mistake she'd made was to become involved with a double-crossing, lying cheater.

## THE BUSINESS TRIP

I wonder how many of you are familiar with this. When you're married to a professional man and he has to go away on business, does he:

- Only find out about it the day before he's going to leave?
- Not know how long he'll be away and not know where he's staying?

Because if he's keeping you so much in the dark that you might as well be a mushroom then he's also ensuring the chances of you finding him out are virtually nil.

Once again to figure this out is easy. If you're planning a trip away do you know where you're staying, when you're leaving or how long you'll be away? Of course you do. And so does he.

Let's have a look at a couple of cases we have investigated recently to show you just what lengths some people will go to in order to use the business trip as a cover for infidelity.

John, a successful surgeon, was in his third marriage to a professional woman whom he had met and had an affair with while still married to his second wife. (This is a huge warning sign: "If he does it with you the chances are he will do it to you." It pays to keep that thought in mind.) So, in effect, my client had first-hand knowledge as to how her husband would conduct an affair. Since we are all creatures of habit I asked her to cast her mind back because he was probably doing the same thing now. Lo and behold, we were right. He flew to a city thousands of miles away, booked into a hotel, instructed the staff to take a message should anyone ring, then hopped on the first available flight back home—where he drove straight from the airport to his lover's house. He then telephoned the hotel, retrieved his messages and called his wife as arranged. Fortunately for our client, "The best barometer for the future was the past," and this prompted her to take a trip to his hotel. When she arrived she was informed by reception her husband wasn't there and had instructed them to take messages.

Brian had started to go out of town on business. His trips were always unexpected but, as he explained to Shirley, it was due to some restructuring within the company that needed his personal attention. Once again one of these trips had come up and he would be away over Valentine's Day, the very day Shirley had arranged a special evening for them to enjoy. Shirley had a very uneasy feeling about this trip. Brian wasn't due back until two days after Valentine's Day but on the special day she couldn't get rid of a persistent doubt and checked the time of the last flight from his destination. She waited at the airport and sure enough who walked through the automatic doors but Brian. She was just about to approach him when she noticed a woman meet him and watched as he got into her car. She followed them and when they pulled up at a set of traffic lights she was directly behind them and saw her husband turn and the color drain from his face as he recognized her.

Now you're probably wondering why these women are clients of mine, having caught their husbands themselves. The answer is simple. Despite having irrefutable evidence they have done nothing with it and have employed me to find out if their husbands are still playing around.

## SEX KIT

Ever wondered why he gets irritated when you poke around in his car or the garage? Well, maybe it's because you could, quite by accident, stumble on his "sex kit" as Joan did.

Even when Richard was out of town, Joan would never drive his car. She had no desire to because she considered her Audi far superior to his Porsche. But on this particular morning she had no choice. Her car had a flat tire and fixing it would make her late for work, so she hurriedly threw her things in the trunk and took Richard's precious car. When Joan arrived at work she took her things from the trunk and noticed the trunk lining was pulled out of place. In attempting to straighten it she noticed a small box like a cash till sitting in the tire well. The box was locked so Joan searched Richard's key ring and found one that opened it. Inside were two packs of Viagra, four packs of condoms, some lubricant and a tube of spermicidal gel. Joan was literally frozen to the spot and her mind went into overdrive. Was this the reason Richard was so paranoid about her going anywhere near his car? It was the most logical explanation. She decided to count the condoms and Viagra and put them all back where she found them and say nothing for the time being.

When Joan got home that evening she went through the garage with a fine-tooth comb and found another stash. This time it was in an old sports bag shoved behind some shelving. According to Joan, she and Richard had never discussed there being any need for Richard to take Viagra. Her finding it was very disturbing as it showed Richard had a secret life.

## Viagra

Viagra was hailed as a wonder drug, the savior to a man's manhood and the solution to relationships that had lost their oomph!

As always let me throw a wrench in the works by telling you how I see the effects of Viagra through my client's eyes. Because Viagra is aimed at men, women are often excluded from the discussion and the decision-making process, which is no surprise. Men are good at having sex but not at talking about it, especially with the one person who is going to be affected the most—their wife.

Usually when a woman has to make a decision regarding her sex life she will discuss it first with her partner. However, this isn't the case where Viagra is concerned. In fact, the pattern that has emerged during my investigations into infidelity is that the man doesn't discuss the situation with his wife but goes to a doctor or wherever he can to obtain Viagra (men's clinics, Internet, etc.). He then uses it for his own pleasure outside his marriage. In these cases the reason the wife finds out is only if she accidentally stumbles across it, as Joan did.

There are the odd few who tell their wives after they've obtained the drug and use one in four tablets for the wife—the rest are used elsewhere. Again this only comes to the wife's attention when she realizes there is very little improvement in her sex life and yet he seems unconcerned, which only causes her to look deeper and discover what's happening to the tablets.

The moral of this story is that Viagra gives men who are prone to straying the ability to continue into their dotage.

It also doesn't surprise me that the makers of Viagra have recently abandoned attempts to use the blue pill on women. For years I've been saying it's foolish to assume that when a woman has an offer, it's just the same as when a man does. We all know men are physically driven—that's why the blue pill works so well for them. However, women are a tad more complex and need physical, emotional and intellectual stimulation. As a result, if these aspects are coming into play in an affair, there is a significantly higher level of risk to the marriage, with an increased chance she will leave for the other man.

## SLEEP DISTURBANCE

I bet you all thought it's men who snore and make unimaginable noises at night, but apparently not. According to many men it's the night-time antics of their wives that drive them from the matrimonial bed and into the spare room—as Chrissie found out. Ben said Chrissie was too hot (her body temperature) and moved out of their super king-sized bed. He moved into the pokey little back room with a bed to match. Chrissie explained they'd had the bed custom made and four people could comfortably sleep in it without disturbing each other.

So what was the real reason Ben moved out? In my experience a lot of men will use an excuse like this to avoid having to face the truth, which is that they are having an affair. Men who move out of the bedroom have usually left their wives emotionally and this is their way of justifying what they're doing. There is no longer any intimacy and they don't sleep with or have sex with their wives. Women who accept this behavior, even if it's not what they want, are condoning it.

## PIN NUMBERS AND PASSWORDS

Why do people have PIN numbers and passwords—for protection and privacy. That's all well and good but if you're in a monogamous relationship why would you have a PIN number on your cell phone your partner doesn't know about, or a password on your computer at home that your partner never uses? I'll tell you why—"If you have nothing to hide you hide nothing."

Trish began to be concerned when her own laptop computer malfunctioned and she needed to complete an assignment so she switched on the computer in her husband's den. She was confronted with a request for a password. Not knowing what it might be she telephoned her husband and politely asked him what the code was. She was taken aback when he flew into a rage, telling her he was far too busy to give her it right then and she would have to wait until he arrived home from work.

Trish was so angry at his response she decided to try a number of options including his name, her name, the kids' names, the name of the dog and so on until she had exhausted every option she could think of. Finally, she keyed in the word "PASSWORD" and access was allowed. What she found was a complete email history of a relationship he was having with a business associate at the other end of the country. She printed it out and placed it in safekeeping for a rainy day. She then shut down the computer and waited for her husband to come home. When he finally arrived she told him she'd managed to have the assignment postponed and she wouldn't require his precious password because her own computer would be fixed the next day.

When she went into his computer the next day in search of more information she found that everything she'd printed off the day before had been deleted. The simple reason for the deletion was that he was concerned he would have to give his wife the password and open himself up to being caught. However, his goose was already cooked.

## DENIALS AND EXCUSES

How can I have such a one-eyed view of infidelity, you may ask? Anyone who believes I think men are the only betrayers is very wrong. As I've said before, not all betrayers are men and not all men betray. However, what I do say with conviction is you can't do a job like mine for as long as I have and keep hearing the same stories and seeing the same evidence and believe this is coincidental. That would be irresponsible, naive and stupid of me.

Ninety-nine percent of the clients I see tell me they have experienced infidelity in their marriage or relationship more than once before they came to me. That shows me very clearly that once a philanderer, always a philanderer. Let me point out that there is a difference between a repeat betrayer and someone who screws up once. If the one-time offender volunteers his indiscretion, actively seeks professional help of his own accord (in other words, you don't have to tell him to get help), is willing to discuss your feelings and talk about your hurt, is patient with you, is prepared to be open and honest and is more than happy to keep you informed of where he is and what he's doing, then the chances are this person is genuinely sorry for his actions. Therefore, the likelihood of this happening again is heavily reduced. There are, however, never any guarantees.

With a repeat offender the only guarantee you have is that he will do it again. The repeat offender will deny, deny, deny to the death—even in the face of irrefutable evidence. In the Bill Clinton/Monica Lewinsky case, had there not been DNA, Bill would still be saying, "I did not have sexual relations with that woman." This is very common behavior among serial betrayers and we encounter it all the time.

I had a client whose husband had a very distinctive car with a personalized license plate. We followed him as he picked up his girlfriend from work and then as they drove to a secluded beach where she performed oral sex on him while still in the car. We documented this and showed his wife and there was absolutely no doubt that the man in the car was her husband.

However, when she confronted him with a verbal allegation, his first response was to deny. When she told him she had hired a private investigator he still continued to deny it was him in the vehicle. He continues to deny to this day he's done anything wrong. Even with so much compelling evidence my client still clings to the possibility that her husband may be innocent for the simple fact that he won't accept responsibility and admit any wrongdoing.

One only has to look at how Hillary Clinton, who is an extremely intelligent woman, has coped with Bill's indiscretions. She only acknowledged the relationship between Monica Lewinsky and her husband because there was irrefutable evidence (DNA) and Bill publicly acknowledged it. The odds are stacked as high as Mount Everest in regards to Gennifer Flowers and Paula Jones but because Bill has never admitted to these indiscretions she publicly refuses to accept he is guilty and always will unless, at some stage in the future, he openly admits it. Constant denial is how serial betrayers get away with it time and time again and therefore there will always be a next time.

When a client calls for my help and I ask the usual question, "Has your partner ever had an affair before?" the response is often, "Yes, I think so. A few years ago I thought he was but I could never prove it." I'll bet this client has had enough proof to know the truth but the proof they are looking for and need is a confession from their partner. However, in my experience not one of my clients has been given a voluntary confession. This deny, deny, deny behavior is very male. Men hate to be wrong or to be seen to be doing wrong—and to be caught is a weakness. Women, on the other hand, when confronted about an affair may initially try to deny it but more often than not a guilty woman will admit her guilt when pressed. That doesn't mean she won't do it again, it just means that women don't have the same degree of arrogance and ego that drives most male betrayers.

## STUPID EXCUSES

When someone is out to deceive you they will come up with the most ridiculous excuses imaginable and if you were not so emotionally involved you would see these excuses for what they really are. But most women, even after hearing these stupid excuses, will find ways to justify them.

> Evidence: You find a receipt from a strip club.
> Excuse: "I just dropped in for a beer."
> Truth: If you only want a beer and not to ogle naked women, go to a bar.

> Evidence: Your husband is seen coming out of a massage parlor.
> Excuse: "I needed some cigarettes," or "I only had a drink."
> Truth: Twenty-four-hour gas stations and grocery stores sell cigarettes. And if you want a drink go to a bar.

Evidence: Your husband has been having an affair and you know who the other woman is. He's promised never to have any more contact but then you find out he's still calling her.

Excuse: "I only called her because she said she needed closure, there's nothing going on."

Truth: If you don't want to speak to someone you don't call her.

Evidence: Your husband is seen out with someone he shouldn't be with.

Excuse: "I was just having coffee with her because she needs someone to talk to about problems in her marriage."

Truth: Since when did your husband become a marriage counselor? And he should have volunteered the information to you first.

Evidence: You find he's made calls every day on his cell to another woman's cell.

Excuse: "She's just a friend from work who I can really talk to."

Truth: Every day is excessive unless there is a legitimate reason such as work and he has volunteered the information rather than you having stumbled across it.

Evidence: Your girlfriend tells you your husband is having an affair.

Excuse: "You know she's jealous of us and she's trying to turn you against me."

Truth: He knows she knows and is afraid that soon you will know.

Evidence: You find numerous calls your husband has made to massage parlors while he's been away on business.

Excuse: "I was bored and just rang them up for a chat."

Truth: These girls don't make their money from chatting on the phone, that's a different service altogether.

Evidence: You find evidence of a visit by your husband to a massage parlor while away on business.

Excuse: "It wasn't for me, Peter used her and I had to put it on my card in case his wife found out."

Truth: Let him know that you'll be asking Peter to reimburse you.

Evidence: You find a receipt for a substantial amount of money for a massage parlor in your husband's wallet with a perfectly legible signature in his name on it.

Excuse: "I was drunk and don't remember anything. I must have fallen asleep."

Truth: They don't charge you for sleeping so why would you pay for something you didn't do? Depending on how substantial the amount there was probably more than one female involved.

Evidence: Your husband decides to leave you.

Excuse: "I just need some space" or "I just need to sort myself out."

Truth: This has got nothing to do with sorting himself out but it is an easy way to have a guilt-free affair. Once the affair is over he may decide he's sorted himself out and will want to come home.

Evidence: You find an empty packet of Viagra but haven't had sex for months.

Excuse: "I've been having some problems in that department lately."

Truth: Unless you have been living in separate universes surely you would know if there had been any problems in that department and considering sex is a joint activity then you should have been part of the decision-making process.

## KEY POINTS

- Receipts, banks statements and credit card bills—when bank statements, credit card bills and cell phone accounts are no longer mailed to home but instead are redirected to his office, you may have cause for concern.

- Too many details—when someone is telling the truth they don't feel the need to go into too much detail. For example, if they were late meeting you for lunch they would simply say they were sorry for being late. But someone who is lying needs to justify the lie to themself and goes into far too much detail.

- Getting defensive—you'll notice that when you ask what used to be a simple question such as, "When will you be home?" he becomes defensive, and if you challenge him he can become verbally aggressive. This behavior is usually a sign that guilt is lurking somewhere. Especially if he is displaying any of the other signs discussed.

- Overly attentive—remember what I said before? Sudden changes in behavior are the tell-tale signs. So, if you have lived with a guy who has never taken much notice of what you wear and what you do, who all of a sudden starts complimenting you on your appearance, beware. Especially if he is displaying any of the other signs we've talked about.

- Talking about a particular person too much—this doesn't have to be in a positive way; talking disparagingly is meant to put you off the scent. Another tell-tale sign is talking about the new woman they've met and their husband or boyfriend or the fact that she's soon to be married. If your partner is guilty of one of these patterns of behavior, beware, because these are usually smokescreens to mask what is really going on.

- The business trip—when you're married to a business or professional man and he has to go away on business, does he only find out about it the day before he's going to leave? Not know how long he'll be away or where he's staying? Of course he knows all of these things but the reason he doesn't tell you is because he has something to hide.

- Sex kit (and other hidden secrets)—ever wondered why he gets so irritated when you poke around in his car or the garage? Well maybe it's because you could quite by accident stumble on his "sex kit," which often contains Viagra, lubricants and condoms. Other items hidden in these areas are prepaid cell phones.

- Sleep disturbance—when men use the excuse of you disturbing their sleep to move out of the matrimonial bed it's more often than not an excuse to avoid having to face the truth, which is that they are having an affair. Men who move out of the bed have usually left their wives emotionally and this is their way of justifying what they are doing.

- PIN numbers and passwords—when you find your access blocked into phones and computers by passwords and PIN numbers, these are signs something is being hidden.

- Denials—there is a huge difference between a serial philanderer and the guy who screws up once. If he denies everything in the face of irrefutable proof and continues to do so, then this issue will never go away.

# three

# WOMEN ARE THEIR OWN WORST ENEMIES

Ask yourself this question: If you knew the guy you were about to marry was a lying, cheating, betraying, immature, deceiving, self-centered, insensitive jerk, would you still have married him? I can hear you say, "Are you kidding? No way." So tell me, why is this kind of behavior all right now?

Women are their own worst enemies and men know it and use that weakness to their own advantage. And why not? You can't blame them because women allow it to happen.

We are caring, nurturing creatures forever running around putting Band-aids on dysfunctional relationships in the hope that they will heal the wounds and that by staying in relationships long enough he will change into a monogamous husband. For God's sake get your head out of the sand. Women need to toughen up and stand up for the right to be treated with respect.

It sounds so easy and if one were to ask women if they respect themselves, of course they would say yes, but in reality that isn't always the case. I see the proof of that lack of respect daily. As a woman who does respect herself I find it the one aspect of my job that causes me the most frustration and sadness. I'm not going to say I haven't been where you are because I have, but the fundamental difference is that in the end I did something about it, whereas 95 percent of my clients don't. I didn't sit back and excuse my husband's behavior because his father died when he was young and his childhood was less than idyllic. I didn't blame the other women for constantly enticing my husband away from me. I did, however, sit back and think, "This has got nothing to do with me. I'm not the one with the problem. I've done nothing wrong." But I initially did something monumentally wrong all right—I believed him, I forgave him and I listened to all the excuses and I thought, "You poor darling. How can I fix this?" So when I say I've been there you'd better believe I have and when I say I know how to overcome this you had better believe that I do.

I'm going to keep on repeating this over and over again until you get it: love is a behavior, not just a feeling. When a man lies to you he is consciously disrespecting you. When he tells you he loves you his words are not enough. When a man lies to you his actions towards you and your relationship are lacking love. You can't gloss over it and make excuses—this is a fact. I find that women, when excusing their husbands' lies, whatever the lies are about, are in the end deluding themselves. There is nothing wrong with being compassionate and supportive but it's destructive to support excuses when you know in your heart that's what you're doing.

So when I hear a woman tell me that apart from the fact she can't trust her husband life is pretty good—because underneath it all he's a good husband, a great father and they have a good lifestyle, that he doesn't mean to be inconsiderate, that he's under pressure at work and is tired and stressed—I want to scream down the telephone, "Pull your head out of the sand; your justifications for his lack of respect just don't wash with me."

In fact, those women who call me because they have a problem have, by justifying their husbands' actions, talked themselves out of the reason for calling in the first place.

When you can justify his behavior so eloquently, does it really matter that you hear a message from a woman on his cell phone that she's missing him, or you read a sexually graphic text message or you can't contact him when he's away on business or you don't know where he's staying because he doesn't either? Of course it matters. You do yourself no favors by making excuses, because when someone has nothing to hide they hide nothing. Think about it. Do you forget where you go? Do you forget what you do? Of course you don't and nor does he, but for as long as you allow him to feed you this line of crap he'll keep on doing just that.

Now I can hear all the reasons why you can't do anything about this and why you have to accept this behavior. You have kids with this man, you've spent 25 years with this man, you can't imagine life on your own, and you can't imagine how you would survive financially. These reasons are all based on fear. Don't think for a minute I'm saying you have to leave but make a stand and take back the power. Men know they have it over women, especially men who are deceiving their wives because they know how vulnerable you are at this time. Don't tell me your husband's not like that. If he's lied to you he's like it all right.

We all have choices. When women make excuses and say they don't, what they are really saying is that they choose to stay in a contaminated relationship because they ultimately think it's easier all around. You have to recognize that by doing that you're not a victim but are volunteering to put your health, sanity and inner peace in jeopardy and I know this isn't what any woman wants to do; you don't need a psychologist to tell you that. We all want to have a monogamous relationship but unless you make a stand you send out a message loud and clear that your feelings don't matter a bit. Most philandering men don't respect their wives' wishes and if he sees that you don't treat yourself with respect either, he isn't about to change. Deceitful, lying, unfaithful men rarely become loving, trustworthy and faithful husbands yet women stay, in the hope that they will.

The answer is very, very simple: If you choose to stay in the knowledge that your husband has lied to you in the past and is lying to you now and has only stopped the affair because he's been caught, and has only gone to counseling because you asked him, then you will experience stress and unhappiness as long as you're with this man. So don't complain, don't nag, don't whine. Accept the choice you have made.

Women are eager to put their case forward as to how they've supported their husbands emotionally, and in many instances financially, to help them get where they are today. I agree that the whole idea of marriage is to share a partnership, to respect and honor and most of all to be committed to each other. However, marriage shouldn't be about martyrdom and it shouldn't be to the detriment of one's self-esteem and self-worth. As an example, one of my clients still makes her husband's lunch every day even though she's lived in a sexless marriage for 15 years (not of her choosing) and knows without doubt of two affairs he's had during their 32 years together. Yet she believes she's a strong and empowered woman who has been terribly wronged and without doubt she has. But she is by no means an innocent player. Her role has been to make it easier for her husband to have the best of all worlds, his only problem is having to listen to a bit of bitching and whining, which men are good at avoiding because they can turn a deaf ear when it suits them.

So what is it about women and martyrdom that seem to go hand in hand? A martyr is someone who suffers or dies for a cause or belief. Martyrs of years gone by were seen as strong people who gave hope and strength to others in their struggle for the right to practice their religious beliefs or speak their mind for a particular cause. Women who are the victims of infidelity and practice a form of martyrdom see themselves as strong women who are suffering for their cause, which is the family unit or their marriage. However, the problem is that this modern form of martyrdom isn't seen as strength by the husband but as a weakness—and a weakness to be exploited.

Then the women try to salvage the fast-sinking marriage by going over the same old ground time after time after time, regurgitating every detail. Yes, it's hard and yes it hurts like hell, but reliving it over and over will not make it any better or any easier. In fact, it is more likely to give him justification for his infidelity because he can say, "God, is it any wonder I never come home when I have to listen to this broken record every day?"

Another classic guilt trip women try to use (but to no avail) is, "You just imagine what it would be like if the shoe was on the other foot. I bet you wouldn't hang around." This is a pretty stupid thing to say to a philanderer because he really couldn't care less which table his feet are under as long as some woman is looking after him. Once again a statement like this is seen as a weakness because you can bet that if he was in the same situation he sure as hell wouldn't stay around.

Then there are the meaningless threats. You may ask why these threats are meaningless and the answer is very simple— it's because they are never carried out.

"Don't worry because from now on I'm going to watch him like a hawk." That's what a client said to me after we found her husband frequenting massage parlors after she had repeatedly told him this was unacceptable. The final straw was when she found a receipt in her son's trouser pocket for both his father and himself. My client had been married for 19 years and for most of those years her husband hadn't wanted to have an intimate relationship with her but she hung in there, living in the hopes that one day he would. When she confronted her husband with the receipt, the only explanation he could come up with was, "We all do things we shouldn't; no one's perfect." So her life sentence is watching his every move. I'm sure you must be thinking: why would you bother? Why would you waste valuable time on someone who is only going to do it again? Why, indeed? But 9 out of 10 women do.

So stop being a martyr and remember you can only change you and no one else. Forget about him for the time being and focus on yourself for a change. You make the choices in your life; don't live it for someone else because you only get one crack at it (that we know of). Otherwise you'll end up living your life like the women in country-and-western songs—standing by your man.

Another example of how women can be their own worst enemies is when they find themselves living in sexless marriages, not because they decided sex is not for them but because their husbands have made that decision for them. The reason given is that they (the husbands) are just not interested anymore. Not only is this a hugely selfish attitude but it is surprising they're allowed to get away with it. The majority of these marriages are of 20–30 years' duration and in some cases the husband and wife still sleep in the same bed, although many men in these circumstances decide to leave the matrimonial bed in favor of a single bed in the spare room.

Jan is one of my long-standing clients (for as long as I have been in business). Jan has been long-suffering and for a decade has lived in a sexless marriage. And before you start telling me that sex isn't everything in a relationship let me remind you of what I said at the outset: If you have a good sexual relationship sex is about 15 percent on the scale of importance. However, if you don't have a good sexual relationship or your relationship (as in the case of Jan) is devoid of sex then that's about 95 percent on the scale of importance. The sad truth for Jan was that her husband was having regular sex with prostitutes and had been for 13 years. The reason why he removed himself emotionally, physically and sexually from Jan was that for those 13 years he had lived out a fantasy by having a string of young women whenever he wanted. In doing so he lost touch with reality (i.e., his 50-year-old wife), and you know that reality almost never lives up to the expectations of the fantasy. So he lost the ability to have a satisfying and fulfilling relationship with his wife.

This book is not about your husband, although it may sound as if it is—it is about you. Please don't get defensive because the truth is hard to hear. The fact is that if you want to change your relationship you have to start with yourself first, from head to toe and from inside out. You have to take the power back and become the sort of person who commands respect and will not settle for less than being treated with dignity and abiding love from the person you've chosen as your partner.

Women will always come up with an excuse or reason for accepting inappropriate behavior in their marriage. Take for instance Kelly, whose husband George frequented massage parlors, spending hundreds of dollars per week. She telephoned with the view that his frequenting prostitutes wasn't as bad as if he were having an affair. I've always had trouble with coming to grips with this way of thinking because sex is sex when all is said and done. What Kelly is really saying is that because there's no emotional connection then it's not as dangerous or threatening to her marriage. Again Kelly, like so many women, is assuming George is thinking how she would think if she were in an extramarital relationship, i.e., it would have to be emotionally as well as physically driven. However, for most men affairs aren't driven by an emotional connection but a physical one and the man is only interested in the person he is having the affair with for sex, which is no different than when he visits a prostitute. So what is the difference between him having an affair with the office assistant and buying her presents and dinners, and paying money to a prostitute? I would suggest none because the result he wants from both is exactly the same—sex.

There may be times reading this book when you might think, "This woman is a shrew." But if I am to be absolutely truthful with you and myself, there's no easy way for me to give you the cold hard facts as I see them. Most of the people who become my clients are in some form of therapy. Whether they are seeing a marriage counselor or a psychologist makes no difference; the fact is they are in serious emotional trouble and, from where I sit, making very little progress—if any at all. When someone is smack in the middle of something as destructive as being continually lied to by the one person they expect to be able to trust, the effects are physically and emotionally devastating. It's easy to pussyfoot around this issue by taking months and sometimes even years (in many cases) to come to some sort of understanding and acknowledgment, but the longer you take to get a handle on it the more damage you're doing to yourself and those around you. There are so many factors to consider including the risk to your health because you don't know your husband's new sex partner's sexual history. So many times children are born out of casual relationships. This can bring about a whole different set of problems, including the possibility that the children of your marital relationship could end up marrying a child of the illicit relationship.

The effect an affair has on the children of the marriage cannot be discounted and don't think for a minute they are oblivious to what's going on. Often it's the children who pay the highest price, especially in marriages of long duration, because over the years they would have noticed the changes in how their parents have interacted with each other. They would have noticed the tension and underhanded innuendo. They would have overheard many a supposedly private conversation.

Remember, certain behaviors are learned and when children grow up in such an environment a boy learns you can have your cake and eat it too. He learns that although he may suffer some minor irritations along the way, all his meals will be cooked, his laundry done and everyone else will think he's an OK kind of guy. On the other hand, the message a girl gets is that this is the way men behave and if you want all the nice trappings it's the price you have to pay. No doubt the next man you meet will be the same, that is, of course, if anyone else will want you—sad but true.

One of the worst things I think people tend to do in situations of infidelity is not to talk about it with anyone. I'm not suggesting you have to go into all the gory details but in saying nothing you are effectively condoning the behavior. I have a client who has had so much proof of infidelity that it's staggering and yet she always finds an excuse to stay. Every time she finds another indiscretion she pushes the line in the sand further and further away. Her continual confrontations regarding receipts and notes found in his wallet and diary show him what not to do in the future and compounds her lonely living hell because her words don't correspond with actions. I've noticed her turn into a bitter and resentful woman and if I have seen it surely her friends and family have seen it too, and yet I know she hasn't told a living soul apart from me. So her husband remains on a pedestal in the eyes of all who know him and he's never had to take responsibility for his actions.

You can see why men continue to betray; the price they have to pay is never high enough.

These women need to strike while the iron is hot because there comes a time (and it has arrived for this client) where spilling the beans would reflect on her credibility. No one would understand why, with all the information to hand over such a long period, she's never told anyone or taken any action before now.

Another sad example that shows how misguided and weak women can be is Tina, who is more than financially secure and if she left her husband would be able to afford more than three homes with money to spare yet chooses to stay in an emotional prison.

I've thought about Tina many times and have come to an understanding of her situation. Like the woman in the previous example, Tina has had more than enough proof of her husband's indiscretions over a long period of time. For a number of years she's had access to his email account and found details of an affair, including messages to and from his lover regarding flight schedules and vacations they were planning when he was supposed to be away on business. We even caught him with his lover in a country hideaway close to home when he had vowed and declared to his wife he just needed time alone in order to sort himself out once and for all. This after Tina had issued the grand ultimatum that if he lied one more time it was all over. But on his return he said he wanted to try to make it work and was committed to his marriage and initiated sex with her. Here was a variation on an old theory that "Men use love to get sex and women use sex to get love." What Karl was doing was not too different in that the sex he initiated with Tina was sending her the signal that he wanted her and therefore tying her to him yet again.

All during the writing of this book my phone has never stopped ringing with people experiencing all forms of betrayal. I had a delightful woman call and ask me what I thought was enough evidence before she took some action. I explained to her that she would have to come to that conclusion herself but I asked her to give me some examples of what had been happening.

> All through our married life my husband Sam has been hooked on the idea of threesomes and group sex. It had never appealed to me but after years of pressure I finally gave in and it was the worst thing I could ever have done because he continually asks for it to happen again, not only with another woman but now with another man and I am sure this request is due to behavioral patterns that show he may be bisexual. On a number of occasions I found him in sex chat rooms arranging to meet both men and women and he has piles of porn magazines in his car.

I let her continue and all the time I was thinking, "What more does she think she needs?" because this isn't what marriage is all about unless both parties have agreed to it without pressure of any kind. In this case it wasn't what she wanted or had agreed to without pressure and therefore he showed no respect for her and their relationship. I continued by asking her if when she got married this was what she expected her marriage to be like, to which she answered, "No, but all men want a threesome, don't they?" I replied, "Not all men but granted, a lot do. However, most married men would only think about it."

She was somewhat taken aback by my answer because for 25 years she had been programmed into thinking she was the one with the problem. This was because whenever she told him she felt uncomfortable in those types of situations he made her feel guilty by suggesting that by not wanting to participate she was spoiling his enjoyment. Surely his behavior and lack of respect was enough evidence to begin with?

Long before you ever encounter betrayal, you need to have some absolutely watertight rules in place about what you will and will not accept. Not what society tells you to accept but what you truly believe you can live with. To believe in your self-worth takes a strong person. Most of my clients think it's easier to stay in a contaminated marriage than to go but I know that with any abuse, in the long run it is easier to leave. Surely it's better to be free to pursue one's own dreams than to stay in a marriage with a man that is a marriage in name only?

When a woman chooses to stay with a man she knows is a repeat philanderer and he does eventually leave, as many do after years of marriage, she feels slighted for putting up with such behavior for the best part of her life. When she finds that all the love and devotion she has shown her husband hasn't changed him and waiting for him to change is a naive notion, she comforts herself by choosing reasons for staying from the following list:

- She loves her husband.
- She loves her children and family.
- She enjoys the lifestyle they have.
- She holds the opinion that all men cheat.
- She could never trust another man.

- Why would she give her husband to another woman?
- Who would want her now?
- Women of a certain social standing need a husband.
- She is financially bound to the relationship.

### KEY POINTS

- Believe in yourself.
- Know your self-worth.
- Have clear boundaries in place.
- Do not accept being bullied or persuaded into doing something you feel is wrong.
- Put yourself first.
- Build a loving relationship with yourself.
- Above all else respect yourself.

# Virtue—a blessing or a curse?

I have chosen to include this subject here not because this is something you have done by choice but because men use virtue against women and yet it is the very thing that throughout the centuries men have wanted in their wives. In years gone by it was seen as virtuous for a woman to enter marriage without any sexual experience and many of my clients have had cause to question this many years down the track.

This interesting fact has come to light due to the increasing numbers of women who, having been married to the same man for 25 plus years, are now the victims of infidelity. They've told me how the very fact that they were inexperienced sexually when they married has in many instances worked against them. It's a fact of life, and one I can back up through my clients' experiences, that the men these women married had far more sexual partners and experience than the virtuous women they married. And so, with the level of sexual experience stacked so heavily against these women, it has been easy for their husbands to manipulate the situation to suit themselves, knowing their wives have nothing to compare them with. This has led to these sexually naive women being sexually conditioned by their husbands. As hard as it is to believe in this day and age, 50 percent of my female clients have been sexually conditioned by sexually dysfunctional men. Dysfunctional may be a strong word to use but these men are living out sexual fantasies and conditioning their wives into thinking this is normal. There would be no problem if their wives were comfortable in participating. However, this is not the case.

A large number of the women I deal with think it's normal for their husbands to place ads in the paper looking for strangers to take part in threesomes. They think it's normal that their husbands want to attend sex clubs while on vacation or say that the only sexual satisfaction they can get is through anal sex. The women do these things not because they want to but because they feel that this is the way to keep their husbands. I know it sounds incredible considering that these women are in their forties and are usually the wives of professional men, but as I have said many times it's all about communication and people just don't feel comfortable discussing sex. There is no doubt that these women are at the opposite end of the spectrum from today's "out there" single female who's had many sexual partners and has analyzed every part of her various lovers' anatomies and lovemaking techniques with her girlfriends.

Many of the women who become my clients have a warped view of sex. They tell me they think all men are unfaithful, all men are into porn, all men demand group sex and all men are sexually deviant, to which I reply that not all men are but if your man is and you are comfortable with it, then that's fine. But if their man is this way and doesn't care whether they are comfortable or not, then I cannot stress enough how important it is not to accept such behavior. They must not roll over and allow their man to dominate but stand up and accept only what they feel comfortable with.

# Guilt trip

Why is it that women who have been constantly lied to, deceived and betrayed feel guilty when they finally decide to take steps once and for all to find out the truth about their marriage? I've had women say to me: "This is wrong, I shouldn't be doing this to him," or "I feel so bad. He would kill me if he found out," and "I can't believe I'm doing this. I feel so guilty."

Knowledge is power and you have every right to know what's been happening in your marriage. It would actually be extremely irresponsible not to because very often it's not just your emotional well-being at risk, it can be your financial well-being along with your physical safety. Don't forget about sexually transmitted diseases (STDs). There are many men who don't use any form of protection and assume that if the woman they are having an affair with is married she will be safe from STDs. They don't consider what her husband may have been doing—is he safe? One of my clients picked up an STD this way, so for goodness sake stop feeling guilty for his actions and start taking responsibility for yourself.

Then I have women telling me how much better they feel just by sharing the problem with someone, taking action and knowing they are no longer accepting his lies. The reason women bury their heads in the sand is out of fear, because if they knew what was going on they would feel obliged to do something about it. The more you know the more able you are to protect yourself. By knowing I don't mean you have to end your marriage there and then but having that knowledge allows you to make choices and to decide what you want to do for your future happiness. Having that knowledge can also help put your mind at rest. It can reassure you that you aren't going crazy. Many women feel this way after confronting their husband because when a woman confronts her husband he will usually try to transfer the blame and make it their fault. He may suggest it's all in their mind and he can't handle forever being accused of something he hasn't done. This is very typical behavior of someone who's caught but in having information and knowledge you don't have to take his guilt on board. Even if he never admits to any wrongdoing (and many don't), at least you know in your heart the true facts—and that's power.

Some clients feel so guilty and ashamed for doing something that they have every right to do that they get a friend or family member to deal with me, another action which is driven by fear. If you choose to live in fear you cannot possibly grow and you therefore give the perpetrator of the infidelity control.

## KEY POINTS

- Cast out your guilt and fear and remember just who is the problem.
- Don't ever have unprotected sex with a philandering husband.
- Never ever feel guilty for standing up for your rights.
- Take the power back because knowledge is power.
- If you need help don't use a relative or friend to telephone on your behalf. Only you know the intimate details of your relationship and it is often those details that are the key for me. Remember that second-hand information loses much in the transfer.

# Leave it to the professionals

If you do suspect your partner of infidelity, whether you have caught him in the past or it's just a gut feeling, don't invest all your time and energy into finding out by trying to do the job yourself because it will end up consuming you.

I have watched women drop dress sizes through nervous energy. It may sound like a quick fix for a weight problem but, believe me, losing weight through stress only leaves you drawn and haggard. I also find that when someone tries to do their own detective work they become obsessed and often focus on the wrong issues, missing vital clues. Someone like me, a professional investigator, brings objectivity to a case, which understandably you cannot have when you are so emotionally affected. Clients become so preoccupied as to their husband's every move that they have no time for themselves anymore and become worn out.

The next and probably most destructive element of trying to play detective is that clients will prolong the inevitable simply by spilling the beans every time they get a piece of key evidence. Instead of keeping quiet until they have a plan of action they challenge and confront their partner, which in turn alerts their deceitful spouse that he is being monitored so he knows what not to do in the future. If you do confront your partner before you have an action plan then you have achieved nothing except to send a message loud and clear that says, "Hey, you go right ahead and have sex with whomever you like and I'll still be here." So don't show your hand until you have evidence (catching them lying is enough) and a plan in mind for your future.

I've lost count of the clients I've interviewed and asked, "Are you sure you've told me everything?" Then, having worked on their case and discussed our findings I've been told, "I knew that already." The importance of releasing all information, no matter how personal or embarrassing you may find it, allows us to achieve optimum results.

Another pet frustration is the client who wants to play junior detective and decides to help by turning up while we're on surveillance. The last thing we want anywhere near the subject is the client, and an emotionally charged one at that.

## KEY POINTS

- Don't hold back information because it's embarrassing to you. We've heard it all before and are non-judgmental.
- Don't try and "out-detective" us. The police don't allow civilians on undercover jobs and neither do we.
- Don't keep spilling the beans; use your smarts. Play it close to your chest until you have the evidence required.

# Intimidation tactics

You finally have a confession after endless denials. The evidence has been too overwhelming for him to keep dodging and he has nowhere else to hide so his only option has been to fess up and admit defeat—he's been having an affair with a married work colleague. Your first response to him is to say: "Right, you get rid of her or I'm telling her husband he's married to a slut." He reacts by saying, "Go right ahead, let it be on your conscience that you've destroyed a marriage. What do you hope to achieve? Why ruin two people's lives? It's not her fault; I'm to blame. Leave her out of this." Reactions such as this are borne out of:

- wanting to protect his lover
- fear
- weakness and cowardice
- utter disrespect

You can see that he wants to protect his lover because he is looking after her feelings over yours, which is really no surprise because he didn't care about your feelings to begin with—otherwise this affair would never have occurred in the first place. He's also afraid of her husband finding out and any repercussions either to himself or his lover.

Weakness and cowardice is obvious because most men will do anything to avoid looking bad, especially in front of friends and colleagues, and will often use intimidation tactics to try and get the accuser to back down. This example shows the husband is planting the blame firmly at his wife's feet in that if she calls his lover's husband and reveals the affair it will then be her fault for breaking up the marriage. He is attempting to divert the attention from his wrongdoing onto his wife. So if you find yourself facing any of these reactions look him straight in the eye and say: "Listen, buddy, you can come up with every fancy maneuver under the sun; you can transfer guilt, shift the blame, minimize and justify, whatever turns you on, but I'm not buying any of it because the fact is you did this; you got yourself into this mess. You deliberately put our marriage in jeopardy. You thought this affair through and executed it—so grow up, be a man and take responsibility for your actions."

He won't expect you to be so direct. You may even throw him off balance but you need to be tough and resolute to deal with his bullshit, because that's all this is, and by getting tough he will know it's pointless trying to elicit your sympathy because that's probably his next avenue of attack.

## THE SYMPATHY CARD

I can still hear Anne's voice when she said to me, "What have I done? You don't think I've driven him to suicide, do you?"

All Anne had been guilty of was confronting her philandering husband about his latest dalliance but David decided to do what he'd always done in a situation like this and play "Mr. Pathetic." He turned on the tears, begged and pleaded with Anne to forgive him because this behavior had kept him out of trouble in the past. By playing on her sympathy he was hoping Anne would forgive him and fall straight back into his arms as she'd always done in the past. The reason this had worked so well for David before was that he wasn't an emotional man at the best of times, so to see him in such a state was upsetting for Anne. Every time he did this Anne believed he was truly sorry for his deeds. But we all have a breaking point and Anne had finally reached hers. This was the fourth time David had been unfaithful (that Anne knew of). However, now Anne was more upset than on the previous occasions because for the first time she'd actually stood up to David; he could see that all his ranting and raving was having little effect. David's parting shot as he stormed out of the house was, "I've had it. I can't take any more of this. That's it, it's over."

Anne was absolutely serious when she asked me if I thought David would take his own life. My reply was, "He's playing with you and thinks he knows you so well he'll know what you're thinking and how you'll react, but to answer your question: No, I don't think he'll kill himself—it takes guts to commit suicide and your husband is gutless."

If you hear responses such as these he's working on the sympathy card:

- "OK, so I lied but that doesn't mean I don't love you."
- "You have no idea how bad I feel."
- "How can you do this to us?"
- "I can't take this anymore."

Don't fall for this manipulation because the minute he gets you back on his side you'll be right back on square one.

Please don't lose sight of the fact that without honesty and respect in a relationship, these being the two essential ingredients, there can be no moving forward.

# Covering his ass by taking advantage of female sensibilities

Often, men who are betraying will sow a seed when they are either running two relationships or you're getting too close to uncovering their secret, because there's always the possibility they will be exposed. What better way to "cover their ass" than by preempting the situation and getting in first with a heart-wrenching story about some terrible physical or emotional illness either to themselves, the other woman, her family or his family? If there is anything that will make a woman back off it's a play on her female sensibilities. This is because it's not in the nature of women (the nurturers and caregivers) to cause undue stress for anyone who is suffering.

This particular type of manipulation is used time and again. Why? Because it works. So if you hear some tragic story from a man you've just met, your husband or partner who continues to take his attention away from you, don't accept all that is said as gospel. Get some facts because you will more than likely find that if he is alluding to having health issues himself, these may well be borne out of the fear that you're getting too close. This type of man only wants part of a relationship and not the whole. On the other hand, if the supposed health issues are about a female friend of his, he is simply playing on your sympathies. With a little research you'll no doubt find she hasn't been diagnosed with cancer, she doesn't have severe psychological problems, she hasn't tried to kill herself lately and her father isn't in the hospital with severe heart problems. In fact, the only person in this story with severe problems is the person telling it to you!

## KEY POINTS

- Don't allow him to shift or divert the blame.
- Be direct and bring the subject back to the fact that he's responsible for his actions, and that for every action there is a reaction.
- If he rants and raves or storms out, keep a cool head at all times and refer him back to the previous point.
- If he tries for sympathy, have your boundaries firmly set and remind him that it's you who has been hurt and no matter how bad he feels it is nothing in comparison to the pain you have been dealt.

# HUMAN NATURE IS A CURIOUS THING

The old saying, "Beauty is in the eye of the beholder," couldn't be more true. It doesn't seem to make any difference if the client is male or female; one of the first things I hear when a client calls is how attractive their partner is. In the beginning of my career I can remember a male client describing his wife as a stunningly beautiful woman and therefore he seemed to half expect her to have admirers everywhere she went. Although he was incredibly hurt by her infidelity he made it sound as if it was something just waiting to happen. I immediately had an image of Elle Macpherson in my mind. I asked for a recent photograph, part of the usual information I collect from a client, which he duly sent to me. I was completely taken aback when I saw the photo of his wife. She was a pleasant-enough-looking woman, a little on the plump side, with short salt and pepper hair. When I phoned my client to say I'd received the information, he said to me, "Well, you can see what I mean, she's beautiful, isn't she?" to which I replied politely, "Yes, she's lovely."

If you think about this it makes perfect sense because one of the vital factors when choosing a mate is physical attraction. What's interesting is that these people believe that everyone else sees their partner in the same light. Nine out of 10 of my clients will make reference to their partner's good looks. For example, a woman will say, "My husband is a very good-looking man" or "My husband is a very charismatic man." Men, on the other hand, say, "My wife is a very beautiful woman" or "My wife is gorgeous."

I will never forget one client who sent me a photo of her philandering, charismatic, handsome husband; he was standing with a group of six other guys at a barbecue. They were all big men with rather large stomachs—I couldn't tell one charismatic man from another. However, there was a particularly unattractive man in the center and when I turned the photo over my client had written on the back: Bob's the one in the middle. This only confirms that beauty is firmly in the eye of the beholder.

Interestingly enough, women take this one step further when confronted with their husband's infidelity. At this stage these men are not only incredibly handsome but extremely clever in their wives' eyes because how else could he have gotten away with it?

But in truth, even if he was as good-looking as David Beckham (whom I consider handsome) he could have all the women in the world throwing their bodies at him but that doesn't mean he has to do anything about it. Only your man is responsible for his actions. No one can make him have sex with them against his will, although it's easier to cope if you believe your poor husband has been seduced into having an affair. And as for him being so clever (what can I say?), if you are on to him, how clever can he really be? This is another way of coping with the fact you've chosen to believe someone who has lied to you. Women try to obtain comfort by shifting the blame for their husband's infidelity. As furious as they are with the knowledge that their husband has deliberately chosen to deceive them, they accuse the other woman of enticing their husband away. Intellectually you know that unless the recipient is willing to be enticed then it can't happen, and though you have your marriage contract with your husband the other woman is under no obligation to you. Particularly if the woman is single, she can do who and what she chooses. Of course, morally she shouldn't be looking for a married man but she isn't your problem. Your husband was the one who pledged to forsake all others and show you respect—so don't lose sight of the fact that, for his part, he's made a conscious decision to betray you. A truly clever man knows better than to ever go down this path so don't give him credit where it isn't due.

I had a client some years ago whose husband started taking Viagra to enhance their sex life. He had it by the truckload, in the bathroom, in the garage, in the trunk of his car and when he went overseas on business he would put the distinctive blue pills into an empty vitamin bottle. Unbeknownst to him his wife was monitoring every disappearing tablet because she knew not one of those pills was used for her. She said to me, "How can I prove he's cheating on me? He's so clever because each time he uses one he replaces it with another." What we have here is not so much the act of a clever man but the actions of a stupid woman.

## KEY POINTS

- Just because you find your partner attractive, don't assume the rest of the world does.
- If your intuition makes you feel that your partner is betraying you, then he's not clever—your unconscious mind has already picked up on the signs.

- Stop putting yourself down and making excuses for your partner's behavior. It's not your fault. He is shifting the blame so let him know that you will not take responsibility for his actions. However, if you do continue to accept this behavior then you have to accept your part in this.

# One minute he's there and then he's gone

I'm sure you will be just as surprised as I was to learn how many men walk out on their wives and families, seemingly with no warning. The first time I heard of this was when a client explained to me that her husband was on medication for depression and had been depressed on and off throughout the 26 years they had been married. But at this time he had actually seemed more settled than he had been in the past. He had been mowing the lawn when he ran out of fuel. He called out to his wife to let her know he was just going to the local gas station to get some more. It was about 20 minutes later that she looked out the window and saw the lawnmower sitting where he'd left it, but no sign of her husband. Twenty-four hours later she was reporting him missing to the police. He had gone with only the clothes he was wearing and, as far as she knew, very little money. Eight months later there had been no contact nor had any money been taken from their joint account. Some ten months after disappearing she finally received a letter from him apologizing for all the pain he'd caused and explaining that he now lived in another town and wouldn't be returning home.

He's now in a new relationship and hasn't formally told his children or had any contact with them. His wife was left to wind down their business and try to put what was left of her life in some semblance of order. We've kept in touch over the years and it's been a long hard haul for her but she's now doing well. Their joint property was granted to her because he wanted nothing. The only explanation she had from him was that he was dissatisfied with his life.

From then to now the cases of this kind have kept coming, but it's interesting to note we've never had a woman do this to her family.

Another client told me her husband went out one Saturday afternoon to buy the weekly lottery ticket and never returned. This wasn't the first time he'd done this in their 28-year marriage, so when he hadn't returned after an hour she had a sinking feeling that history was about to repeat itself. Although this man had a very responsible job he was prone to mood swings, had gone off with other women in the past and had stayed away for months at a time but he would always return, saying how much he missed her. For my client this time was the last straw. She explained to me that the most frustrating part of trying to cope with this was that there was never any explanation from him as to why he did it. As it's not a common situation to find yourself in, those around you won't fully understand what you're going through and in turn won't be able to offer much help, which leaves you extremely vulnerable and isolated. For his part he could see the devastation he caused but it was never enough to stop him.

## Men who leave with somewhere and someone to go to

I'll never forget Denise's call. She said:

> I've been married to an absolute bastard for 30 years. He's just walked out telling me he doesn't feel we have anything in common anymore. I wonder when he came to that conclusion. He's been a damn bully all our married life. He'll bonk any female who crosses his path and I have put up with hell for years, and now he just

> decides he's going to go and start a new life. What about
> me? What am I expected to do? He swears up and down
> that there's no one else; he just can't stand being around
> me any longer. I bet you've never heard of this before.

Before I could answer Denise was off again:

> He's not getting away with this. I haven't spent the
> last 30 years doing his dirty laundry just to sit back and
> let that bastard dictate to me. I have no idea where he's
> gone to; he wouldn't tell me but I need you to find out.
> He's got to come back here this weekend to pick up the
> rest of his clothes so I thought you could follow him
> from here and see where he goes.

To respond to Denise's statement ("I bet you haven't heard of
this before"), I think it's fair to say I've heard everything before. It's impossible to do my job and not hear these sorts of
stories over and over again. That's where my knowledge has
come from.

We did follow Denise's husband that weekend and he led
us to a modest apartment in a trendy and expensive part of the
city. A few minutes later a woman arrived, driving his other
vehicle, and punched in the security code to the underground
parking area. One of my investigators had found a superb van-
tage point on an adjacent street with uninterrupted views of
the subject's balcony and lounge area, where it was very easy
to observe Denise's husband and his lover. It turned out that
they were very serious about their relationship and had been
for quite some time, so much so that they'd bought property
overseas some months earlier and moved there to set up home
only a few days after we watched them.

Jen was another long-suffering wife and had been married to
John, an international airline pilot, for 32 years. His lifestyle
gave him enormous opportunity to play the field and he took

full advantage of it. Like most men who deceive, John wasn't particularly good at it and Jen was on to it right from the start. Jen knew of five affairs, all of long duration, that John had conducted and countless one-night stands, but, like Denise, she'd done nothing about it other than relentlessly berate him, using threats that never materialized. John got to the point where he just turned off, knowing she would never kick him out as she threatened to do. As long as he could cope with the tirade of abuse hurled at him, life wasn't too bad. The end came when John started having an affair with a senior member of his cabin crew and finally told Jen he'd had enough of her constant moaning and was moving out to an apartment in the city. Truth was, John had fallen in love, or so he thought, and was moving in with his new love. However, that didn't last and he moved out one week later. John now lives alone and sees them both periodically.

The statistics say that only 5 percent of such relationships last the test of time. Women like Denise and Jen who live with men who are repeat offenders in the infidelity stakes run the risk of their partner leaving. Choosing to stay in a relationship riddled with infidelity must have a payoff, and for these women the payoff was lifestyle. But men who have essentially been dating all their married life and are at an age where they are prepared to take a gamble only leave if they have somewhere and someone to go to. It is important that women put more emphasis on not how much love they give to their husbands but how much love they are receiving in return. Women believe that by hanging on to him at all costs and loving him, he'll do the same, but this behavior doesn't guarantee faithfulness or even love being returned.

Jerry Hall springs to mind as a woman who's traveled down this path, loving and constantly forgiving Mick Jagger through all his betrayals. Not his children or even their history together was enough to deter Mick from his philandering ways. Mick and Jerry are no longer together but Mick found somewhere soft to fall.

Not all women are as fortunate. Jerry Hall is beautiful, famous, rich and successful in her own right and therefore has a greater range of opportunities than many of my clients, who often don't see themselves as strong, attractive and vital women. Women cling to the commonly held belief that if they can sit it out long enough one day he will grow out of his philandering ways. I'm afraid to say, ladies, that you are deluding yourselves and in doing so you are essentially giving away your life to a man who will never change no matter how much time you give him. It's true that leopards don't change their spots just as frogs don't turn into princes. It's a sad fact that once a philanderer always a philanderer, so don't waste precious time waiting for him to change; it won't happen because he doesn't want it to. This sort of behavior is a habit and these men have always been like this in varying degrees. Whether you have chosen to acknowledge it is up to you.

Think about it like this. Do you start every day with a cup of coffee? If you do, that's a habit. If someone said you weren't allowed that coffee you would realize how important it is to you. If you were then told you would never be able to have coffee again I'm sure you would think, "I could do that, but really what's the issue? It's only coffee." So before long, you would revert back to your morning coffee.

Men who betray don't put any more emphasis on their infidelities than you do on your morning coffee. Your partner doesn't see it as a big problem—it's you who does—to him it's only sex, it doesn't mean anything. And he's still looking after you (financially) and he hasn't left you (yet). Just like you with your coffee he may be able to stop for a while but eventually he'll revert.

The reason he can and often will leave is because he's disconnected from you. If he had any care and consideration for you at all he wouldn't have behaved like this to start with. So just as you could change from coffee to tea, if he had wanted he could have concentrated on his life with you rather than pursuing other women.

The only way to change a habit is if you really want to and are 100 percent committed. You must acknowledge you are changing for yourself and how it will better you and not someone else—otherwise it won't. It's like an alcoholic going to AA because his wife has asked him to stop drinking—it's not going to work because it's his wife wanting him to stop, not him.

So if you are living with a serial betrayer, don't spend the rest of your life trying to change or even trust him but concentrate on trusting yourself to make the right decisions for you in the future.

# Girl power

I have been saying for years that women are not so different from men when it comes to their desire for sex. Men believe they have the monopoly in that area, which is partly out of arrogance and partly from social conditioning. They really believe their partner would never cheat on them. However, women are not as demure and naive as men think because when it comes to infidelity, women are head and shoulders above men in terms of the planning and execution of an affair.

Just as many women betray their husbands as men betray their wives. The only difference from my point of view is that I work mainly for women. That tells you one thing: women get away with it far more than men do, and there are many reasons for this. Firstly, women today have far more independence than they ever had in the past. One behavioral trait in betrayers is that they are opportunists and with so many women out in the workforce they are now faced with opportunities not available to women 30 years ago. They don't just sit around waiting for their men to come home. In fact, quite often it's the other way around.

Women today are emotionally and socially stronger than ever before and know that if their marriage does break down they have the wherewithal to survive. Also, contraception plays a major role, giving women sexual freedom. Women are also staying sexier for longer (hallelujah) than in the old days. In the past, if you weren't dead at 40 you certainly weren't seen as a sexual being, but now we're living longer and with hormone replacement therapy (HRT) there is no reason why anything has to change. I have had many clients in their sixties and seventies with very healthy sexual appetites.

# The revenge affair

Women are notorious for the revenge affair, more so than men ever realize. A woman will plan her affair; she will usually have a back-up plan and a girlfriend who will cover for her. Women never ignore their intuition but men have suppressed their intuitive skills to the point where they rarely use them. Again, this is to a woman's advantage when covering her tracks. If you likened the sexes' intuition on infidelity to a runaway train hurtling down the tracks, a woman would sense the danger before hearing the train but a man would probably only know the train was there when it ran him over.

Sally was married to a man who lied like a dog. She had been suspicious of him for years but could never prove anything . . . well, anything that would satisfy her. However, she did have copies of his cell phone bill. On checking these it became clear there was a number he phoned consistently. In fact, it occurred at the same time as he was pulling out of the driveway each morning. What disturbed Sally was that this was the number of her best friend, so she asked for one of our investigators to park outside her friend's house to see if Mike arrived. It was obvious from what we saw that the reason for Mike phoning as he pulled out of the driveway was to check if the coast was clear at her end—in other words to see if her husband had left for work. Moments after Sally's friend's husband left, Mike pulled up and when she opened the door for him she was still dressed in her nightie. Old Mike fondled her breast as he walked through the door.

Sally asked us to observe for a few more days to establish a pattern so that, once and for all, Mike wouldn't be able to lie his way out of this situation. Sally was furious and said: "I'll show the silly old fart. He's not going to treat me like a fool and get away with it. He'll rue the day he walked through that door, and I haven't finished with him yet."

It was a couple of months later that I got a call from Sally and she sounded like a different woman; there was laughter in her voice and she told me she'd sorted Mike out and now he was walking around with his tail between his legs. But she wasn't about to stop there—Sally wanted revenge. So she put an advertisement in the personal column looking for a man to have discreet sex with and to her amazement she got 200 replies from one small ad. They ranged in age from 19–80 and she narrowed them down to 30 potential lovers. Then, every day when Mike went off to work, Sally would get all preened up and go out to interview her potential playmates. She was having the time of her life. In the end those 30 became five and those five became her lovers. Laughing, she said to me, "Men are stupid. Mike thought he was so clever having his little fling right under my nose but he would have a fit if he knew what I was getting up to with not one but five fantastic men. But he would never consider I would do this—what a fool."

# Friends and allies

The reason a lot of women get away with infidelity is because they have an ally in the form of a close girlfriend. It's so easy for a woman to say, "I'm going to meet Debbie after work, do some shopping and have a bite to eat." Most men wouldn't bat an eye because it's the most natural thing for a woman to say. It's exactly what Anne did.

Debbie and Anne had been friends since high school, had similar lives and, now with their children growing up, would occasionally go off on a girls' weekend together. It was on one such weekend that Anne met Tony. One thing led to another and they ended up embarking on an affair. Debbie and her husband owned a beach house close by but because of their busy schedule they never got to enjoy it. Debbie gave the key to Anne so they could have a private place to go to at lunchtime. Sometimes, when Debbie's husband was out of town, she would let Anne use her house and Debbie would go out for an hour or so.

My experience shows that this kind of behavior is very common and the reason women can use a friend as an ally and get away with it is that they are natural communicators. They talk on a deeper and more intimate level, sharing confidences and thoughts. Men are aware of this and don't think anything of it.

# Who's the boss? Wives who blame the other woman and confront her

I've had so many clients do this, and I consider this behavior embarrassing and humiliating. It never seems to make the situation better; the wife never gets what she wants. In fact, on the whole, it seems to make matters worse because the lover either denies any involvement with the husband, which is incredibly frustrating, or she goes into so much detail it only causes more pain. Then the wife loses dignity in front of the other woman and in doing so gives the lover the power. So her plan has totally backfired because the whole objective of the confrontation was to show her husband's lover who's the boss.

In many cases what usually happens after the confrontation is that the lover runs straight to the husband complaining about the verbal and sometimes physical abuse she has just endured and he takes her side against the wife. This only adds more fuel to the fire and makes the wife even more enraged. The vast majority of my clients blame the other woman for enticing their husband into infidelity and believe he would never have crossed the line if he hadn't been seduced.

Dianna always had suspicions that something was amiss with her husband and she was usually right. On this occasion it was someone at his gym. There had been women in and out of her husband's life from day one of their 23-year marriage. Dianna had endured this behavior, believing it was the norm (all men cheat), but that way of thinking had never stopped her from confronting the women in the past and it wasn't going to stop her now. Dianna truly believed her husband would never leave her, so in a sad sort of way she derived comfort from the fact that following her confrontations he always ended the affairs and stayed with her. And it was true that the only reason he ended the affairs was because she found out but it wasn't enough to stop him from having affairs.

When we found out who the other woman was, Dianna was relentless in pursuing confrontation. She waited for her husband's lover outside the gym one evening, then all hell broke loose:

> You are nothing more than a cheap little slut and if
> you know what's good for you you'll leave my husband
> alone. He doesn't want you; you are just like all the other

cheap little sluts that take their panties off for him. If he
loves you so much why is he still with me? I bet he tells
you we don't have sex; that's what he told the last one
but let me put you in the picture—we have plenty of sex.

Dianna hadn't left the parking lot before her husband's lover
was on the phone to him giving him a piece of her mind because he'd told her he and Dianna slept in separate rooms. He
spent the rest of the day comforting his lover, which only
caused more devastation for his wife. Since then Dianna has
shown up at her work and harassed her on the phone—all in
a misguided bid to show her she is the boss.

## KEY POINTS

- When you marry you have a contract with your husband.
  When he betrays you and breaches the contract then he's
  the one at fault, not the other woman.

- It is unbecoming to go yelling at your husband's lover. In
  doing so you are disrespecting yourself and in his mind
  that gives him justification to disrespect you further.

# Boundaries

I find it fascinating how people's perceptions of betrayal dif-
fer. Bill Clinton had a very clear view that oral sex did not con-
stitute betrayal because it wasn't penetration and he's not
alone, but many of my clients are vague when it comes to
defining this. In the end it comes down to boundaries—what
you will and will not accept as behavior conducive to a truthful and trustworthy relationship. If you put these in place prior
to your marriage then there is no doubt and no misunderstanding in either of your minds that should these rules be broken the injured party can act on them. A good example is that
before you receive your driver's license you take a test, which
allows you to show that you understand the rules for driving

your car. Failure to follow those rules when driving your car can have serious consequences and this should be no different to the boundaries drawn up between two people entering into a relationship.

Very few couples actually discuss the nuts and bolts of what is really important to them before getting married. Considering this is supposed to be a lifetime partnership it appears that more discussion goes into the color of the flowers at the wedding than the boundaries they will accept. You might say, "I can't stand it when you fart in bed," but when it comes to the bigger issues, i.e., your views on infidelity, you are afraid that if you say what you really think you might not make it to the altar. This is incredible when you think about it because we are talking about your life and future happiness. What better way to find out what his boundaries are than by observing his reaction? At least when you do have the courage to sit down and discuss the details no one can say after the event, "I didn't know you felt that way and I wouldn't have gotten involved if I had known." At least this way you and your partner are under no illusions as to what you will and will not accept.

From a private investigator's point of view domestic peace-of-mind work can be the most frustrating because most couples haven't addressed these issues. Therefore, if one or the other finds themselves having to deal with infidelity no amount of evidence is ever enough because the boundaries of both parties are unknown. Just about every client wants to know that their partner has been caught in the act, yet for us to say that your partner has checked into a hotel room with another woman and spent the night with her is, according to most of my clients, not enough. They say to me that if they don't have actual proof, i.e., a photograph of sex taking place, then he will just lie, say nothing happened and accuse you of going crazy. Well, of course he will. He's not about to say, "Yes, honey, I took my secretary out for a fantastic dinner, then back to my palatial hotel room for a night of rampant sex."

Forget about obtaining a photograph of the sex act. Instead, consider what he was doing with her in the first place. And if it's OK with you that your husband lies to you about what he's been doing, because clearly he has, you need to ask yourself, isn't the simple fact that your husband spent the night in a hotel room with another woman and never told you enough?

### KEY POINTS

- Know in your mind exactly what behavior you will and will not accept from your partner.
- Make sure your partner has a clear understanding of your boundaries so that there is no confusion.
- If you do discover that your partner has lied to you and you are going to confront him then you need to be prepared to act.

In the following cases it is interesting to note that all these women thought they were at fault for asking a question they had every right to ask, and yet what is even more interesting is that they were willing to accept whatever explanation their husbands gave. When I pointed out that to believe what they had said could be a risk, in all cases there was stunned silence on the end of the phone before they quickly sprang to their partners' defense by reiterating the explanations they had been given. Yet it is very simple. All of these women have proof that their partners have lied to them, so why are they willing to believe their partners' explanations?

In this book I'm going to keep repeating things over and over again until you get it: love is a behavior, not just a feeling. When a man lies to you he is consciously disrespecting you. When he tells you he loves you the words aren't enough. When a man lies to you his actions towards you are unloving. You can't gloss over it and make excuses—this is a fact. When women excuse their husbands' lies, whatever the lies are about, they are deluding themselves. As I've said before, there is nothing wrong with being compassionate and supportive but it's destructive to support excuses.

Take, for instance, Rebecca, whose husband Steve told her he was going on an office night out but never came home. He telephoned the following morning to say that he'd had too much to drink and had gone home with Mike and stayed at his place. This wasn't the first time he had stayed out all night after one of these "office bonding" sessions but Rebecca had always believed his stories as to why he hadn't returned. The nagging doubt that persisted for Rebecca was that he would only call the following morning after the fact and that it was only a 20-minute taxi ride home. That particular morning Rebecca decided to telephone Mike to see if the story stacked up, only to find a voice message saying Mike was out of the country and wouldn't be back for two weeks. When Rebecca questioned Steve about this he became aggressive and said, "I will not be interrogated by you. What is this, the Spanish Inquisition?"

Rebecca's reason for calling me was to ask if I thought she was overreacting as she had no evidence. But, in actual fact, she had all the evidence she needed. Marriage is a partnership based on respect and Rebecca knew Steve had lied to her. The only reason you lie is to cover up for something you have done. He had also become aggressive, which is another sign of guilt, and he could give no reasonable explanation for his behavior—because there wasn't one.

My response to Rebecca was to ask her if lying was OK in her marriage, to which she replied, "Of course not." I cannot stress enough that couples need clearly defined boundaries as to what is acceptable to both of them in their marriage, and a universally held view is that lying in order to deceive is not acceptable. So what more proof do they want when they know their partner has lied to them?

Hannah and Chris had been married only three months when Chris started visiting his ex-girlfriend two or three times a week for what he claimed was coffee and a chat. Knowing that Chris had been very heavily involved with this woman before they met, Hannah didn't feel comfortable and asked Chris not to see her again. She explained to Chris that if she was just a female friend then an occasional visit would be OK but this woman had been his lover for many years and the closeness of their previous relationship left her feeling decidedly uncomfortable. Chris said he fully understood her concerns and promised he would have no further contact with his ex-girlfriend. A few weeks went by and Hannah was beginning to feel a little better until one day she couldn't contact Chris on his cell phone and her anxieties came flooding back. So she drove by the ex-girlfriend's house and sure enough Chris's car was parked in her driveway. That night Hannah casually asked Chris if he'd heard from or spoken with this woman since he'd promised not to have contact and he said, "No, I haven't seen her since we had our chat."

Hannah called me to ask if we could find out for her what was going on inside the house. I replied that we couldn't see through walls and she didn't need to know what was going on in the house because Chris was already showing a lack of respect by choosing to lie only two weeks after promising not to see his ex-girlfriend.

So once again the question of what your boundaries are and what you are willing to accept must be called into question.

It's not a question of what other people are willing to accept but what you personally are comfortable living with.

For some women boundaries are stretched beyond any reasonable limit so in essence they have no boundaries and more importantly their partner knows this and uses it to continually abuse and disrespect them. Women who continually move the line in the sand further and further away show by their actions that they don't respect themselves either.

This is a common occurrence in my line of work and is apparent with couples in long-term marriages. They have been through counseling (usually at the wife's request) and now they are off to the lawyer's (usually at the wife's request), where she is going to draw the very last line in the sand. Her husband is going to go along with it just as he has before because he knows that the tide always comes in to wash the line away

Tina and Karl from Chapter 3 (Women are their own worst enemies) are a prime example of a couple where the wife has lost all self-respect and her boundaries have stretched so far and wide that she can't remember where most of them are.

Tina and Karl are wealthy beyond most people's imagination, and any split of matrimonial assets would leave them both in a position where they would never need to work again. So Tina decided she had drawn a line in the sand once too often and headed for the lawyer's office to get rid of him once and for all. As the lawyer drew up the various documents Karl used his trump card and in a show of emotion said he still wanted Tina and was so sorry for what he'd done that he wanted one last chance, and if she gave him this chance he would prove to her that he meant it. In front of the lawyers they both declared she wouldn't accept any further indiscretions and he would abide by his promise. Within days of that meeting he was back to his old tricks and to this day they are still together. Periodically they meet with lawyers to draw up more meaningless documents.

## Male boundaries

I have thought long and hard about this particular facet of male behavior and I've come to the following conclusion, which seems to make sense (or at least it does to me).

Over the years I've been astounded at how many men take their lovers back to the matrimonial home, and more importantly into the matrimonial bed, with never a care or thought as to what this action means, not only to their marriage but to their wife. For men the home represents an asset, an investment or simply bricks and mortar, and that leaves a man with a far less emotional link to the home than that of a woman. Men rarely describe the place they live in as their home but as their house, their piece of real estate or their castle. The words used to describe it reinforce a lack of emotional attachment. Since evolution women have had an intimate bond with their home because it's where they nurture their families while their husband or mate hunts and gathers for their needs.

Because men don't share the same intimate bond with the home as women it's easier for them to betray in the matrimonial home. Women, who have such a personal connection with their home, wrongly assume their husbands do as well and would never consider betraying them at the heart of the family. When I suggest such an occurrence may have happened or could happen, I can hear the indignant tone in my clients' voices. They tell me their husbands would never take anyone back to the family home but the truth of the matter is that this boundary is broken all too often.

◆ ◆ ◆

In the previous chapter, I discussed women who thought it was less threatening to their marriage and position if their husbands visited prostitutes rather than have an affair. This thinking is based around their assumption that there is no emotional connection, and they are correct, but the flaw in their assumption is that men are suckers for a "damsel in distress." When men visit prostitutes they enter the realms of fantasy and often become victims of the hard-luck story. The hard-luck story generally revolves around the girl needing money to get out of the industry or needing cash to set herself up in her own apartment so she can pursue her education or career. She may suggest she will be his special girl, and it would amaze you how many intelligent men allow themselves to be taken in by these women. You could say it's the "knight in shining armor" or "Pretty Woman" fantasy, but much nearer to the truth would be the man's lack of self-esteem and confidence, which allows the girls' flattery to take hold so easily. That applies to most men who betray and covers all socioeconomic groups and job types. Remember, these girls wouldn't choose to be intimate with these men unless there was money involved. It's their job to make these men feel special. The girls are there for one reason and one reason only and that is MONEY!

On a number of occasions we've been employed by men who have fallen into this trap in order to establish what their newfound friend is up to in the apartment they have provided for her and what educational courses she's attending. In all cases their new friend was making good use of the apartment, majoring in sex and had far more than one special friend.

This is Jack's story.

The man on the other end of the phone had a friendly and cultured voice and introduced himself as Jack. He went on to explain that he worked for a large law firm and had been happily married for 27 years. My first response after listening so far was to wonder why on earth this man was calling me. Until Jack said he'd fallen in love with another woman and was seriously considering leaving his wife for her, that is. I suppose it's fair to give Jack credit for admitting to falling in love with another woman. And in his mind he was doing the honorable thing by ending his marriage. Then he told me the other woman was a girl he'd met at the massage parlor he frequented. Jack admitted he'd been helping her out financially as well as paying for her services, but he assured me it was only to help her get started out on her own because at the moment she lived at home with her mother and baby brother. I gave Jack all the pearls of wisdom I had for a situation like this and wished him all the luck in the world because he would need it.

Obviously nothing I said sunk in because about two months later I got a call from a hospital where Jack was on the line, sounding very down in the dumps. The first thing he said was, "God, I wish I'd listened to you; I've totally blown it. You wouldn't believe what has happened."

Jack went on to say he'd paid the deposit on an apartment and furnished it for the woman at the massage parlor and paid the down payment on a car, then he'd gone on a skiing vacation with his wife and family. Although he was going to tell his wife he was leaving her he couldn't ever find the right moment. However, on the skiing trip Jack suffered a terrible fall and shattered his leg, which put him in the hospital and in traction for six months. He was beside himself with worry and wanted me to make sure his new love was coping at home alone. My investigators only had to watch for a day to find out that although Jack wasn't enjoying the fruits of the little love nest he had helped provide, other men were.

Jack isn't the first and won't be the last to fall for the damsel in distress line and he needn't have worried too much because her new soft-hearted sugar daddy is an accountant who is sure to follow where Jack left off.

# HOW TO SPOT
# A CHEATER
# FROM 1OOO YARDS

This section of the book is a must-read for women young and old. These simple tips could save you from emotional and financial disaster, and untold stress. In other words they could actually lengthen your life because, as I noted earlier, living with high stress levels for a prolonged period can seriously reduce your life expectancy.

## Actions speak the truth, not words

We've all heard the expression "Talk is cheap" but that's pretty hard to remember when someone you adore is whispering sweet nothings in your ear. However, in order to be protected from a con man—whether he's after your money or your heart—there is a great test you can do. If he's the kind of guy who talks a lot about what he's going to do and in particular about what he's going to do for you, treat him like a television set and put him on mute. Don't listen to what he says he'll do but see what he actually does. An example of this is when someone you meet says they'll call you tomorrow. A week goes by and you hear nothing, then they call and say they have been so busy they haven't had time to call. Let's be honest, that's rubbish; it literally takes seconds to dial a number but the number of people who will excuse that behavior is huge.

Then you go out with someone and have sex together, but two weeks go by before you hear from him again. He comes up with all the reasons why he hasn't been able to contact you. But let's be honest: the truth is that if you really want someone you'll contact them come hell or high water, just as if you broke your leg you would go to the hospital and have it fixed rather than hobble around for a day saying, "Oh hell, I haven't got the time."

Another example is when you're in a relationship with a guy and you've arranged to go out for dinner but he suddenly cancels, saying he thinks he's coming down with the flu. But, as chance would have it, one of your friends sees him at a restaurant with another woman. When you confront him his first response is to lie and say it wasn't him but finally he admits he was there and gives you the story that he'd arranged to have dinner with his ex-girlfriend and felt you wouldn't understand if he told you the truth. It was easier for him to lie than tell you the truth. Again, the proof of his feelings is in his actions, not his words.

## When someone shows you who they are, believe them

People will always show who they are in the beginning. It's just that often we don't see it either because we're caught up in the excitement and emotion or we choose to ignore it. Instead we come up with excuses such as: "Once we're married everything will be fine," but the paperwork doesn't change anything because if there is a problem in the beginning of a relationship it's usually that problem which will end the relationship. Women in particular will often spend their lives trying to fix things they have no control over. That's why, when you meet someone and you find in the beginning they have a behavioral problem or a character flaw, you need to think long and hard about whether you want to pursue the relationship. If you choose to continue then you have to take responsibility for your actions.

You meet the man of your dreams: he's single, has a good job, money in the bank and loves kids, animals and you, so it seems. As your relationship progresses you discover he's not as single as you first thought, although he's quick to explain that the reason he told you he was single is that the relationship he is in has been over for ages. It's really a matter now of just moving out, oh . . . and telling his partner of the last five years that their relationship has been in trouble for the last few months because this will undoubtedly be news to her. So you figure he didn't want to hurt you by telling you the truth and once he moves out and leaves her and moves in with you your problems will be solved. He tells you he loves you and thought he was doing the right thing and he'll never keep anything from you again. You accept his reasons and move in with him. Three years later you start noticing little changes. He's not as attentive as he used to be. He gets quite aggressive and short-tempered with you, especially when you ask him where he's been or is going. You start to notice he can't go anywhere without his cell phone and even takes it to the bathroom with him. One night you couldn't find him but then you saw him in the yard, standing in the dark and talking on his cell phone. Your mind flashed back to when you first met him and remembered how he would often call you late at night and you could hear road noise in the background. Eventually you find out he's been having an affair for the last year.

If you go back to the beginning of this story you'll see very clearly that he showed you who he was when he met you. He was already in a relationship and looking to set up another one. The question you should have asked yourself is, "If the relationship was so bad why hadn't he left already?" because remember, "If they do it with you they will do it to you." Humans are creatures of habit and this guy was just doing what he's always done. That's why I say, "The best barometer for the future is always the past."

## There is no smoke without fire

If you hear a rumor about your new partner, especially from family and friends, take heed because the saying is true: "There is no smoke without fire."

These are the cold hard facts you don't want to hear, especially when you have just met the most amazing person and everything seems so right. The last thing you need is me telling you that you've got it wrong but the reason these people slip past your guard is because the moment your emotions come into play is when a large part of your common sense goes out the door. If you weren't touched on an emotional level you would not only see quite clearly what the problem is but you would be listening as well.

## Wandering eyes

We all like to look at what we perceive to be an attractive person. That is a healthy and normal instinct. However, a problem arises when a man stares at someone else and the attention is taken away from the person he's with. Then it becomes a warning sign.

I recently had a meeting with the husband of one of my clients and it took me just 30 seconds to see that she had a problem. We met in a hotel foyer and he could have told you where every female was in that room. He couldn't seem to help himself. I found his behavior extremely rude so imagine what it must feel like to be his partner and multiply that feeling tenfold. I don't even think he was aware of what he was doing; he was talking to me but his eyes were all around the room. It's not much to expect that the person you are with gives you their full attention as a sign of respect. If your partner regularly shows signs of this behavior you have cause for concern. The same can be said of men who are forever commenting on other women in front of their partners. Again this shows a lack of respect, which goes hand in hand with infidelity.

## KEY POINTS

- Take notice of what he does, not what he says he will do. A person's true intent lies in their actions, not their words.
- Don't discard your intuition. If you have doubts about someone, take your time and get to know the person first.
- Keep an open mind, listen and learn and don't think you know someone when you have only just met them.
- Don't accept disrespectful behavior. There is a line between appreciation and showing disrespect to the person you're with.

# Beware of the wolf in sheep's clothing

Cases like the ones you are about to read occur far too often for my liking. They always involve a vulnerable woman and a middle-aged man. The profile of the victim in these love crimes would be a woman who has lost her husband either by death or divorce, usually after many years of marriage. She will be financially secure with property and money in the bank and will not have realized how terribly lonely she has become until the wolf enters her orbit. These women will still have children around but at this time in their lives they are very rarely living at home and may have families of their own. Once the wolf gets his foot inside the door he will then work at every opportunity to alienate the victim from her children and family. This is to stop any form of opposition to him and she in turn will rarely listen to her offspring's protestations, as she will feel they don't understand her need for male companionship.

There is a lesson to be learned here. In many of the cases we have investigated it has been the children who have been on to the wolf long before the victim but have felt powerless to do anything in the face of their mother's misguided happiness. However, in a number of cases it has been the family who have employed us to unmask the wolf.

The profile of the wolf is that for all his years of working he actually has very little or nothing at all to show for it, bar money-making schemes, a high opinion of himself—and delusions of grandeur. He is what I would call a "would-be-if-he-could-be-but-never-will-be person."

He'll have a whole list of reasons why he's down on his luck, and in his mind it will always have been someone else's fault that the business venture went bust or he lost his home. He can be described as a financial opportunist and often presents himself either as a charming rogue or a rough diamond— the exact opposite of the former husband or partner of the victim-to-be; I call it the "Lady Chatterley syndrome."

Some wolves don't have to do anything for their keep because many of the victims are so desperate for love and companionship they shower their wolf with gifts and money. The wolf (who really has no feelings for them) treats them with disdain and contempt, yet still the gifts and money flow. The following cases are good examples of this behavior.

Margaret placed an advertisement in the local newspaper for a handyman and with only one reply she allowed Frank to tidy up her small yard and do some decorating around her apartment. Margaret continued to find work for Frank, who she always paid in cash, and this arrangement continued for some considerable time. They would always finish the day's work with a chat and a cup of tea and during one of these conversations Frank told Margaret he didn't like apartment living. Margaret was beginning to have some feelings for Frank, who was the exact opposite of her late husband, a refined academic, and so she decided to move out of the apartment (which she really loved) and buy a house with some grounds. There were two reasons for this move—Frank didn't like apartment living and she was beginning to run out of things for him to do.

Frank was a landlord. He told Margaret he owned a home but was renting it out because it was way too large for one person to rattle around in. At this stage everything was platonic but Margaret always made sure there was plenty of cold beer in the fridge and added a little extra to his pay to allow him to bet on the horses. But this was about to change.

Margaret was used to attending the theater and ballet and wanted to take Frank out with her. But she was appalled by his clothing (his usual attire was black shorts and a T-shirt) so she bought him a whole wardrobe of clothes in a style she thought appropriate. Margaret never saw Frank wear the clothes and later he told her he hated them and had given them to a thrift store.

Once the new house was purchased Margaret had plenty of work for Frank but the house was quite some distance from

Frank's house and he complained that his old car wasn't big enough to carry all his tools and materials. Margaret bought him a bigger and better vehicle on the understanding he would pay her $50 per week until the sum was repaid. By this time Frank knew he was on to a good thing and began to up the ante by asking Margaret for large sums of cash on the pretext that he needed new tools and equipment. Following each request Margaret would go to the bank and withdraw the money. Margaret also paid for all their outings and gave him regular amounts of cash to spend on himself. All this was over and above the cash she paid him for work carried out on the house and yard.

Two things happened that should have soured the relationship. The first was when Margaret became seriously ill and called Frank to come over and take her to the hospital. Frank refused and was extremely abusive and cold. Margaret, in immense pain, managed to raise the alarm with some neighbors who called an ambulance. Frank refused to visit her but this didn't dampen her feelings.

Then she began to realize Frank never stayed over on a Friday night and was unreachable at weekends. Although she visited his house he was never anywhere to be seen. When she questioned him he questioned her sanity by saying, "You must be senile, woman, of course I was there."

He began to constantly criticize her and it appeared that everything about her annoyed him intensely and yet Margaret was in love and his behavior was overlooked—however, not to the extent that she didn't ask for my help. This came about because after his constant criticism of her he had stopped all contact and refused to take her calls or visit her. Her request was to have him watched from Friday afternoon to see just where he went on the weekend.

On Saturday morning we followed him from his lodgings to a large home some 25 minutes away. He drove the car purchased with Margaret's money into the driveway and picked up another woman of similar age to Margaret, went to the supermarket (where we noticed the shopping cart was filled with beer and cigarettes). At the checkout stand, and later at the gas station, it was the woman who paid. Further checks revealed that the woman was the sole owner of the property and she had been in Frank's life for five years and had left the property to Frank in her will.

When Margaret learned of the other woman she was devastated but still wanted Frank and told me she would have jumped out of a plane without a parachute if he'd asked her to, so deep were her feelings for him. In her mind this was a relationship, but unfortunately no one else would see it that way, least of all Frank, who saw her as an easy source of funds.

Not only had Margaret been funding his lifestyle with cash but Frank was drawing a paycheck and taking whatever his second victim offered as well.

The tragedy of this story is that Margaret, despite visiting lawyers (and spending more money), would take him back at the drop of a hat.

Valerie was a woman in her late fifties who had lost her husband in a car accident, which left her a very wealthy woman by anybody's standards. As a result of stress, she had become ill to the point of being unable to drive. Then along came Allan. He was the mechanic who had serviced her car and was interested in buying it when he found out she could no longer drive. When it came to paying for the vehicle Allan couldn't afford the full amount but suggested that because Valerie couldn't drive he would offer his services to take her wherever she wanted to go as the balance of the payment. Valerie was prepared to accept this deal and so the arrangement began.

Allan had a "rough diamond" kind of appeal, very different from Valerie's husband. The relationship became physical within a few weeks because Valerie had been starved of affection for such a long time. This allowed Allan to gain the financial maximum from the relationship in a very short time. Allan told Valerie he'd been living with his mother because his recent divorce had cleaned him out financially and his ex-wife had taken it all and left the country. Allan appeared to be all the things Valerie had dreamed of and, true to his word, took her where she wanted to go. Valerie fell for his hard-luck story in a big way.

After her husband's death, Valerie had been contemplating a vacation, and when Allan played his sympathy card and complained of not having been able to afford a vacation because his ex-wife had left him financially strapped, she jumped at the chance of time away with him and booked and paid for a vacation. In all they went away three times in the short period they were together, with Valerie paying every last cent. She later told me that in their time together he never even bought her as much as a cup of coffee.

During their third trip away Allan said there was an old school friend who lived about 300 miles to the north of their vacation home. Aware of Valerie's dislike of sitting in a vehicle for long periods he said he would rent a car (Valerie paid), go see his friend and be back in three days. Of course he didn't have any cash so Valerie gave him $1000, not knowing that it wasn't an old school friend he was going to see but his ex-wife, who he'd been in constant contact with and with whom he was on the verge of reconciling.

Part of Allan's plan was to get Valerie to buy him a home, and on their return he went into overkill in order to please her.

But he was also becoming moody. He said it was because he was desperate to move away from his mother but in truth the moods were because he only had weeks before his wife was due to return and he needed a home for her to move into. Allan was playing games with both of them but Valerie was completely unaware and purchased a small cottage for Allan. He asked if she would decorate, furnish and clean the property. She duly obliged, using some of her own furniture that Allan had taken a shine to. However, it was at this point that she noticed he wasn't as available as he had been. When she asked why he said the relationship was moving too fast for him and he needed space. This puzzled Valerie, especially as he had been so intense just a few weeks earlier.

Of course the reason Allan wasn't seeing Valerie was because his ex-wife had moved into the new house and he'd promised her they would reconcile. This was the point where Valerie came to me and asked me to investigate him.

Valerie cannot accept the fact that Allan has done this to her. She believes it isn't physical despite the fact that Allan and his ex-wife are living together and have been seen out together. Allan had not only lied to her about who he was visiting while they were away on vacation but had stayed at his ex-wife's apartment during the visit.

There are similarities between Margaret and Valerie's stories in that both women can't see that they played their part in allowing this to happen by buying affection. Both are going to play the victim by saying quite vehemently that they will never trust anyone again. Therefore they could possibly spend the rest of their lives as very lonely women when there is no need. They should have done their homework first and exposed Frank and Allan for what they were—frauds.

When they get what they came for, these frauds suddenly cool off emotionally, become quite aggressive and can leave without a moment's notice, refusing to communicate in any way, shape or form. This is their way of cutting dead the relationship and leaving their victim heartbroken. They then go on to squander their ill-gotten gains on projects that have a snowball's chance in hell of succeeding before beginning the search for their next victim.

Should you find yourself in this position, or if you are at the start of a relationship where you've noticed some of these warning signs, then do yourself a favor and don't accept at face value the hard-luck stories you're being fed. These men know how to play on a woman's sensibilities and vulnerabilities. You won't be the first and if he has his way you won't be the last. We normally find a whole list of previous victims who have lost not only their hearts but also their homes and futures.

◆ ◆ ◆

The number of clients who want me to sort out their financial woes long after the event are too many to count and the vast majority have become victims because they have jettisoned their financial brain in favor of their emotional one.

When you enter into a relationship treat it as if you were starting a business, especially if you are in an independently strong financial position. Remember that when a company decides to take over another company they don't do so without checking the financial standing and business systems of the company they intend to take over. It's called "due diligence," and if it's not carried out, "Let the buyer beware."

When a financially independent woman meets what she considers to be the perfect man she should realize there is very little difference between entering into an emotional venture and a business venture, except that with the emotional venture comes the chance that both your emotional and financial well-being are at stake.

Kate's story is a lesson for any financially independent woman. We can all get wrapped up in the romance, the lust and the buzz of meeting someone new and not see the signs (and there are always signs). For Kate they were there right from the start but she chose to ignore them.

At 54 and a widow, Kate had her own business and a string of properties. She was charming, self-assured with a great sense of humor but lonely and, as she pointed out, emotionally vulnerable. Friends had invited her to a local nightclub many times and having refused so often she decided one night to placate them by arriving unannounced—and that was the night she met Bill.

Bill was some 10 years older than Kate but he was an excellent dancer and listened intently as, with the aid of a few glasses of wine, she told him all about herself—a big mistake. She felt guilty that she had monopolized the conversation and began to ask him about his life but she obtained little from him except that he was a widower and property developer. They agreed to see each other the following week and then began a relationship. She still knew very little about him; it was as though he had no history at all. That was the first real clue that maybe there was more to Bill than met the eye.

On weekends they would go away to a country lodge and each time it would be Kate who paid for everything because Bill was always waiting for funds, which never materialized in time for him to pay his share. That was clue number two. This might happen once but more than that and it should have set off the warning bells. Instead, Kate began to feel sorry for Bill, who was living in a partially finished house not far from her own, so she allowed him to move in with her despite the fact that she knew so very little about him.

Soon they were working on a deal to sell most of her properties to fund an even bigger deal that would net them a large sum of money. The profit on this deal was huge and at this stage Bill persuaded Kate not to place the funds in her own account but to open a joint account with individual signing rights so they could take advantage of further deals. This account was now flush with cash and wide open to abuse. This was clue number three but again it was missed.

It was about this time that Kate's daughters decided to voice their concerns to their mother. They argued that their collective gut instinct was that their mother was being set up for a financial fall. At this stage Bill had never contributed a cent towards housekeeping or outings, and began to use the account without consultation, withdrawing hundreds of dollars a day.

When Bill got wind of Kate's daughters' disapproval he decided to move out and return to his half-built house, because the truth was that he was happy living there in semi squalor and had never been happy living with Kate. He had done so only because he was after her money.

To Kate's knowledge Bill still had property developments of his own, which he had said were about to be completed, so, even though he had left, she saw the time coming when they would pool their joint assets and live together. But then things began to change. She noticed Bill had withdrawn a six-figure sum of money, which, when challenged, he said was to complete his own house project and he would repay the money with interest when it was completed and sold. What Kate didn't know was that Bill was a bankrupt who had four ex-wives and owed creditors in excess of $250,000. The reason he had borrowed this large sum from the account was not that he needed to finish the property but to pay off creditors who were threatening to force a mortgage sale if he didn't pay up.

By now most of the profits had gone from the account and he was becoming less and less the charming rogue and more and more aggressive and distant. Kate admitted later that they had never actually consummated their relationship in the conventional way. But despite this he again managed to persuade Kate to fund a property investment, which would require all the remaining funds from the joint account plus remortgaging her property. The warning bells were ringing so loud they would wake the dead, and Kate's daughters pleaded with their mother not to go ahead but it was all to no avail. Kate signed in good faith without reading the small print.

What Kate had signed was not what she had thought it was. According to Bill, the development had run into trouble and the money had been lost. Kate then found that Bill was unavailable when she called and to this day she's never seen him again. She has lost virtually everything and is endlessly fighting him through the courts at even more expense.

## KEY POINTS

WARNING SIGNS

- A man in his fifties who enters your life with a whole load of excuses as to why he has no assets;
- A man who asks for money, even if he says it's a loan;
- A man with no history (there is always history);
- A man who always seems to have no money at the crucial moment;
- A man who is always waiting for the big pay-off, which never materializes;
- A man who suggests you invest in a business venture but doesn't feel it is necessary for you to know any more;
- A man you wouldn't normally be attracted to but for whom you make an exception because you're so lonely.

WHAT NOT TO DO

- Don't lose sight of who you are. Does this person have the same values, morals and ethics as you?
- Don't be indiscreet about your financial affairs.

- Don't try to buy affection.
- Don't think you can change who he is by changing what he wears.
- Don't dismiss as jealous gossip warnings to be careful because he's got a bad reputation.
- Don't discard the concerns of your immediate family and close friends. Remember, they are looking at the situation from an unemotional viewpoint.
- If you have a niggling, uneasy feeling even though you are very attracted to this person, listen to your intuition—it's rarely wrong.

PROTECTION/REMEDY

- Never sign anything without first taking it to your lawyer.
- Ask questions about him—get as much information as you can and check it out.
- If money or business ventures come into this relationship, ask for his permission to do a credit check. If he refuses that is in itself a warning. ("If you have nothing to hide you hide nothing.")

# Financial betrayal

For some of my clients betrayal comes in many forms. Emotional betrayal is bad enough but when combined with financial betrayal the situation can become too much, with, in some cases, a breakdown in mental and physical health.

Lana, Rachel and Lydia thought they knew their respective husbands well but in actuially not one of them had a clue about the emotional and financial blows their husbands were about to make them suffer until it was nearly too late. Each of these women became aware of the financial betrayal about to occur only when attempting to discover if their husband was having an affair.

Lana's husband Barton was 63 and a prominent man in the city. Now approaching retirement Barton had become involved in one of the city's largest educational establishments as a way of bridging the gap between his full-time business life and retirement some two years away. They had been married for more than 35 years and their children were all married and living in various parts of the world. Lana knew Barton was struggling with the idea of retirement, so when he said he needed three months to clear his mind and visit Europe's art galleries and historical sites, she went along with his needs and supported him as she had done throughout their married life. Barton left for Europe, leaving Lana to run her business.

The first warning signs arrived with his credit card statements. Although Lana knew Europe was expensive she couldn't help but notice that bills for meals were so high that no one person could have eaten so much. As the weeks went by the bills continued to roll in and Lana expressed to me her concerns that Barton might just have someone with him. We discussed who it might be and the only person she could think of was a visiting female professor from Germany with whom he had spent an awful lot of time at a university function some six months earlier. He'd never mentioned her again and hadn't given Lana any reasons to doubt him. However, after making a number of telephone calls to Europe we had a description of his traveling companion confirmed by staff at two of the hotels he had stayed at, and sure enough it matched the German professor.

Up to this point Lana was still convinced it was just a friendship and they had joined up with each other for a few days to enjoy a mutual interest in Roman architecture, but further investigations showed they met on his first night in Europe and had been together ever since. Lana was deeply wounded by his deceit and it took some days before she was able to come to terms with what had happened. When she did it was a different woman who approached the task of finding out exactly what was going on.

Barton was still only six weeks into his twelve-week vacation and Lana wasn't about to let those six weeks pass without finding answers to questions and concerns she had obviously buried deep within her. She began a systematic search of all their properties, offices, garages and lofts to see what she might uncover about her husband and the German professor. I was given the order to search for all assets in his name and to continue to compile a dossier on his European trip for later use if the need arose.

It didn't take long for both Lana and myself to make discoveries that rocked her to the very core. She had so far managed to hold up through the knowledge of his emotional deceit but the discoveries we made took her close to despair. During a search of his office, in the very back of a small closet, she found a small cupboard. Inside was a document folder containing correspondence that showed he had been salting away funds and had set up a number of trusts into which properties and other valuables had been deposited. Legal documents showed he had been systematically planning a future without her for some eight years. My own investigations found that he owned two properties which Lana had no knowledge of—and to her horror both were owned jointly with the German professor.

However, the piece of paper that caused the most despair was a single page in his own handwriting where he compared the options of staying with Lana or starting a new life with his German professor. It was entitled "I've Been Thinking" and concluded that Lana was worth very little despite 35 years of marriage. One line in particular said, "What has she contributed to our wealth apart from being a mother to our children, tending the house and running a small business that makes a pittance? When we split then that cannot be worth more than 20 percent of my wealth," with the words "my wealth" underlined!

On arriving back in New Zealand, Barton didn't return home but set himself up in a motel where he said he was taking further time out to decide on his future. Surveillance showed that in fact he spent no time at the motel whatsoever but all his time with the German professor at one of their homes. The German professor had in fact obtained residency some years earlier and had traveled on the same flight as him to Europe.

Rachel and Heath, both in their late forties, had been married for 20 years and had two teenaged sons. Heath ran a successful financial services company while Rachel was his support. She looked after their sons and helped entertain his many clients. To everyone including Rachel, Heath was seen as the perfect husband and provider.

Then, during one of their many dinner parties for clients, Heath announced he had arranged a two-month surprise summer vacation trip for Rachel and the boys to see her parents in the UK. Rachel was delighted that Heath had gone to such lengths with the arrangements but wished he was going with them. Heath told her he'd taken on a number of new staff and in his words, "The business is expanding rapidly and it's very important that I'm on hand to bed them in."

Rachel was so busy preparing for the trip she missed vital signs that under normal circumstances her intuition would have picked up on. One week later she and her sons left for the UK.

Before leaving, Rachel had agreed with Heath that she would contact him every other day either at the office or at home depending on their itinerary. For the first week she managed to make contact as agreed. But on the second weekend one of the boys had broken a bone in his hand, so she called home but there was no answer. Having tried the office with the same result, she called his cell, which was switched off.

The following day she tried all three phones but with no luck. By this time she was becoming concerned and wondered if Heath had had an accident or had become ill. On Monday morning she called his office to be greeted by a new voice, one that seemed highly protective of her husband's whereabouts. When the young woman realized she was speaking with Heath's wife her voice was even icier and more protective than when they had begun their conversation. Finally, Rachel was able to make contact with Heath, and asked where he had been over the weekend. His answer was that he'd been in and out and the battery of his cell had died and he couldn't be bothered getting a new one until this morning.

On two occasions during the following week Rachel called at night and on both occasions there was no answer. This was beginning to worry her, so she called at 2 a.m.— again no answer. The following day she called in the late evening and he was out, but he answered his cell saying he couldn't talk but would get back to her in a few minutes. When he did call back he was clearly out near a road as traffic could be heard driving by. His excuse was that he'd been in a business meeting and was now outside the hotel. Rachel was beginning to have concerns about his whereabouts. It was the following day when the pieces of the jigsaw puzzle began to fit into place.

Rachel decided to call his office and was greeted by a friendly voice, not the icy tones that had greeted her last call. She asked the receptionist if Heath was available, only to be told he'd gone to lunch with Rochelle, his new assistant. Rachel asked if it was Rochelle she'd spoken to a few days ago and the receptionist said it would have been because Rochelle had been answering the phones while she had been away on vacation. Rachel then telephoned his cell and it was turned off. She finally telephoned home and there was no answer.

It was at this point that Rachel called me to ask if I could assist her. She began by telling me her story so far and gave me the address for surveillance purposes. It was then that I asked if she had a monitored alarm, to which she replied yes. My suggestion to her was simple: request a movement report from the alarm company, which would tell us when and at what time the alarm was activated and de-activated. Within 24 hours I had a copy of the monitored alarm activations, and sure enough Heath hadn't been home when he said he had. In fact, the only time he'd been at home after Rachel's first week away was the previous lunchtime when he was with his new assistant. They had stayed for two hours. The report for that same night showed the alarm had not been activated.

We began surveillance outside Heath's office. When his vehicle emerged from the parking lot on our first day, he was driving and in the passenger seat was a young red-headed woman who looked about 20 years of age. They powered away from the junction in a very expensive sports car (certainly not the vehicle description we had been given) and arrived at a luxurious new apartment complex with views over the ocean.

Heath stayed the night and drove Rochelle to the office the next morning. At lunchtime that day Heath and his assistant drove to the family home and entered. Once again they stayed for a couple of hours and then returned to the office.

We checked ownership of the apartment and sports car and found that both belonged to Heath. We also carried out asset checks on Heath and completed a full business survey, which produced some extremely worrying results. We reported to Rachel what we had found but she was in denial and said we must be mistaken. We therefore asked her to arrange to speak with Heath each night at home for one week so we could prove what he was up to. We stressed to her that she shouldn't give him any reason to be suspicious.

Each night that week Heath would drop off his assistant at the apartment, drive home, answer Rachel's phone call, leave his home and return to the apartment where he would stay the night and then drive his assistant to the office the following morning.

Rachel left her sons in the care of her parents and returned home. Booking herself into a hotel she arranged a meeting with me to try and come to terms with the emotional and financial situation we had uncovered. Before our meeting Rachel rented a car and parked within viewing distance of her own home, and sure enough Heath and Rochelle drove up in the sports car, stayed for an hour and a half and departed for the office. When the coast was clear she entered her home and found the bed rumpled. She couldn't understand why he would bring someone back to the house when he already had a secret hideaway, unless it was for some perverse reason. She also found a remote control, which she hadn't seen before. She immediately recognized it as a garage remote and so off we went to the beach house. As the door slowly opened it revealed a space filled with what could be called "big boy's toys," including two jet skis, a pair of mountain bikes, water skis, a small motor boat and a whole pile of boxes filled with Rochelle's personal belongings. Rachel was stunned at the expensive toys Heath had bought because many of them were things he'd promised his sons but had always said they couldn't afford.

This was all the proof Rachel needed. She visited a lawyer armed with our information, which showed Heath's business was in dire trouble and his spending was out of control. In fact, he was spending as if he had no financial problems at all. Rachel began the long journey many women have to travel when their husbands wreak financial and emotional havoc on their families.

We found that Heath had in fact met Rochelle two years earlier and during that time she'd gone on overseas business trips with him, where he had spent lavishly on hotels, food, wine and gifts, including designer outfits and jewelry. He continued to maintain his excessive lifestyle until he filed for bankruptcy. He was asked to explain his extravagances and come to a settlement with Rachel, but such was the tangled web of financial deceit that it took a forensic accountant to show just how he had deprived his family financially.

Throughout her married life Lydia heard all the gossip about her husband Doug and various women with whom his work brought him into contact. Like many women who are the partners of influential businessmen, Lydia did her utmost to maintain her position in society and be seen as the dutiful wife, who backed her husband to the hilt. She had all the trappings of her position and enjoyed these fully. When the subject of her husband's infidelity came up from time to time she did her utmost to minimize, rationalize and justify the excuses for him staying out later than he should, not being where he said he was or the gifts and purchases on their credit card statements that never came her way.

So when the rumors began about Doug and his exotic-looking secretary, Lydia fell back into the role of dutiful wife and justified these rumors as the words of people who were jealous of her husband's position at the very top of his industry. After all she'd met the secretary at a number of functions and found her to be quiet and deferential. She didn't appear to be any threat to Lydia despite her being attractive and 30 years younger.

Unfortunately for Lydia the persona portrayed by Aisha at the various functions was in stark contrast to the one that attracted Doug. Behind the deference lurked a smart, sharp woman who knew exactly what she wanted and a powerful man like Doug could give her all those things. She'd known Doug was a player and found it easy to snare him.

While the rumors persisted, Lydia went about her life as though nothing was amiss. She wasn't overly concerned because she and Doug shared everything (or so she thought), from their home and boat to rental properties, trusts and shares.

When Doug walked out on Lydia he and Aisha had already set themselves up with a multi-million dollar home overseas. Doug had also decided he no longer wanted to be based in his home country and moved the company's seat of power offshore. Lydia was totally unaware of what was going on. Doug was a master at hiding things and in the eighteen months prior to leaving had, with the help of his accountant, removed Lydia as the beneficiary of family trusts, changed the trustees and siphoned money into overseas bank accounts.

The catalyst for Lydia to call me was when Doug moved out of the matrimonial home and set himself up in an apartment, where he played the part of a recluse so well there appeared not to be any other woman in the picture. Despite Lydia's denial that anything was going on between her husband and his secretary, the old adage that there is no smoke without fire had us watching Aisha. Surveillance on her home was about to be called off when we saw her old car pull out of the driveway and set off in the direction of Doug's factory and on arrival disappear out of sight behind the main building. We waited for her to come out and although a number of vehicles departed (the factory ran a late shift), including a silver Mercedes sport, Aisha's vehicle wasn't one of them. We called our colleague parked close to Doug's apartment and asked if he had anything to report and received a negative response. However, being a car buff, he noticed a distinctive Mercedes sport had just pulled into the underground parking garage and, guess what, it was the very same vehicle we'd seen at the factory.

At 5 a.m. the following morning the Mercedes, with Aisha at the wheel, drove from the apartment and back to the factory, where Aisha picked up her own car and returned home.

The harsh cold facts of Doug's affair stunned Lydia but she had only scratched the surface when it came to bad news. Lydia confessed she'd always let Doug handle the financial side of their relationship, although on closer scrutiny it appeared it was more a case of her having absolutely no say in what happened to their money. Doug had issued her with an allowance for housekeeping and personal expenditure but he handled all other expenditure. This had allowed Doug free rein and he'd used this to essentially embezzle money from the marriage partnership and deny Lydia access to family trusts by removing her as the beneficiary and making changes to the trustees. Lydia also had to face the fact that her husband had made claims on property and valuables that were hers through a deceased estate. As well as facing a major battle to keep her head above water, there were emotional and personal issues plus a lengthy court battle to contend with in an attempt to sort out what was, under law, rightfully hers.

Because of the complexities of this case and Doug's ability to manipulate the financial circumstances to his benefit, Lydia found she was in no position financially or physically to keep the home that had been the cornerstone of their lives for more than 35 years. She was devastated at losing the family home and moved to a much smaller property where, having now recovered from the double blow of losing her husband and home, she is building her own life and exploring new possibilities—without, for once, the controlling figure of Doug.

It could be said that the clients whose cases are described above had lifestyles they took for granted and they should have taken more care to ensure their financial futures were in no way compromised. However, what is perfectly clear is that these women all played a full and equal part with their husbands in building the matrimonial estate, making it what it was at the time of separation.

In my experience there was no way any of these women took for granted the lifestyle they were living. Yes, they may have overlooked or missed important signs, which suggested their husbands were betraying them emotionally, but never financially. All three husbands had gone to such great lengths to hide their betrayal and had carried out their deceptions over a long period of time. The length and depth of the deceptions had a specific purpose, which was to ensure their wives felt safe and content while they continued to undermine the very trust these women believed was the foundation of their relationships. If it hadn't been for the simple seeds of doubt sown in terms of emotional uncertainty, all three would have had no prior knowledge of the financial betrayal that befell them.

What is interesting in all three of these cases is that the men went to extraordinary lengths to hide their financial betrayal from their partners and that the financial betrayal was the key to ensuring their future with the new women in their lives. What should be of concern to all three mistresses was the degree to which each of their men deceived their wives. How would you feel as the mistress of one of these men, knowing that you, too, could be treated with exactly the same lack of feeling as the women who had given them unfailing support through the best years of their lives? Does a leopard change its spots? I think not, therefore the new women in their lives must surely be concerned as to how long they will last and how secure their financial future will be. I would advise each one of them to take great care to ensure they have financial independence because as they age and the novelty wears off, they may become less attractive and the chances are that these men "Having done it with them will do it to them."

And if that saying isn't sufficient, try this one on for size—
"The best barometer for the future is the past."

◆ ◆ ◆

How do you protect yourself against financial betrayal?

- Consult a family court specialist and set out exactly what you consider to be the assets of the marriage. Prepare the documentation thoroughly so as not to waste time and money.
- Make sure that joint signatures are required on checking accounts.
- Have all bank statements sent to your home address.
- Credit card statements should also always be sent to your home address.
- Know who both your bank manager and accountant are.
- Regularly have independent checks on any trusts, especially when you and your children are beneficiaries.
- Ensure that mortgages are as they should be. We regularly see clients who find their husband has taken out loans against the family home or has refinanced the home to fund other ventures.
- If you have any suspicions, have someone look over your husband's assets—especially for property.
- You should consider having a clause to include your approval on the sale of any property you consider a risk.
- If you have shares or bonds make sure they haven't been sold.

# Cheaters on the Web

Modern technology—friend or foe? Betrayal doesn't have to be physical. With the advent of the Internet, people are becoming hooked on chat rooms, dating and pornography sites, and the time spent pursuing their fantasies or looking for a sexual adventure is time taken away from their partner. One of my clients became so infuriated by her partner spending so much time viewing pornography on his computer that she ripped it out, threw it in their bed and then said to her husband, "Why don't you sleep with it as well?"

The danger of the Internet is that people can pass themselves off as anyone or anything, and misrepresentation is rife. We have recently had four separate cases where four people misrepresented themselves and the four people they were dating did the same. The common denominator was that they were all married and their partners knew nothing of their betrayal!

Chat rooms and dating sites are open season for liars and cheaters and we find that relationships escalate at a much quicker rate when conducted over the Internet because people have such easy access to the other person, no matter what country they are in. When someone is out there looking for love or sex they have to accept that the risks of running into a predator or serial philanderer are high and that could be the price they pay.

A recent client found a profile of her partner on a dating site in which he depicted himself as never having been married, never having had children and, as she described it, a whole load of other lies and bullshit. She found his password, entered his site and altered his profile so that anyone entering it would read the truth.

Sarah was a genuine first-time user of a dating site. She responded to Brett's profile mainly because he said he was also a first-time user. Sarah and Brett hit it off right away (talk about beginners' luck!). The relationship progressed quickly and, because they were both in there fifties, Sarah didn't think they should wait before moving in together.

After only a few weeks of living together Sarah noticed Brett was missing from the bed in the early hours of the morning. While going downstairs she could hear him tapping on the keyboard of the computer but when she entered the study Brett hurriedly logged off. This gave Sarah an uneasy feeling and so when Brett went out later that day she tried to enter the computer but was blocked by the requirement of a password.

Sarah was feeling rather anxious and so decided to set up another profile, calling herself Barbara. She wanted to see if Brett was still looking for a "date." To her surprise he took the bait, hook, line and sinker. He wasn't even subtle and used exactly the same lines he'd used on her. Sarah scanned a photo of an attractive 30-something female from a magazine and sent it to Brett. He replied immediately and suggested they meet, and a time and place was arranged.

All the next day Sarah felt sick wondering what excuse Brett would come up with in order to meet Barbara. His excuse was so plausible that if Sarah hadn't known the truth she would have believed him. Brett set off for his meeting with Barbara, and Sarah thought for someone who was normally a sharp dresser he didn't look too smart that morning. In fact, it even crossed her mind he might not be meeting Barbara but actually doing what he'd told Sarah as an excuse. But unbeknown to Sarah, Brett had placed a complete change of clothes in his car. Sarah hurriedly got ready for her appointment and arrived at the shopping mall just before Brett. She was there to see him arrive in a completely different set of clothes and carrying a bunch of flowers. She was able to observe him circle the food court like a shark looking for its prey as he tried to spot Barbara among the throng of lunchtime diners. After watching him for a further 10 minutes she left in disgust, drove home and threw his belongings out.

This should have been enough for Sarah, but Brett charmed his way back not once but twice until finally she found him with another woman and this time she learned that "The best barometer for the future is the past."

◆ ◆ ◆

Another interesting example of Internet dating and deception hit worldwide headlines just recently when a United States soldier was found to have become engaged to or was dating via the Internet nearly 50 women while being married. Most of these women used a dating site that dealt with tall men over six feet three inches, yet the guy in question was only five feet nine inches. He received hundreds of gifts and thousands of dollars from these women and was only found out when he actually met one of the women and she discovered he was lacking at least six inches.

This is a sad case and heartbreaking for the more than 50 women who fell for his lies and deception but I had to laugh when I read his excuse for not being the six feet three inches he'd said he was. He told the woman that in carrying out numerous parachute jumps the pressure of the landings had reduced his height to five feet nine inches!

Do I need to say more?

**KEY POINTS**

- The Internet is a haven for emotional cheaters.
- Profiles in dating sites are like resumes! Check them out thoroughly.
- If you are going to meet someone you have met on the Internet, make sure you do it in a very public place and tell a friend where you are going.

## Financial love cheaters on the Web

I've already warned you of the emotional love cheater who is out to steal your heart or, if caught, break his wife or partner's, but there's another type of cheater out there. They inhabit the same chat rooms and dating sites but they're not really interested in you for your looks and sexual preferences (although that's where they'll start) but for your money, property and any realizable assets you have. I've covered this kind of person in a section of this book (Beware of the wolf in sheep's clothing) and what to watch out for, but on the Internet it's more difficult. You may be dealing only with words. Even pictures can be of someone else and not the person to whom you think you're talking.

This form of cheater will be looking for women or men of independent financial means, and it's amazing how much information they can gain prior to any meeting. The reason for this is simple; the Internet is so informal people tend to open up far more freely than they might in more formal surroundings. Sending photographs of your house or discussing the type of business you own gives the Web predator the opportunity to decide if there are pickings to be had.

Watch out for the man or woman who, after a reasonable period of time during which you have formed an Internet relationship, gives you a small hard-luck story, which normally requires you to send them $100, just to get them through the next few days. They will generally repay this immediately but that's the test to see if you will go along with their scam. If you don't, you'll find their interest in you will cool very quickly. If you do, you'll find their needs continue.

An interesting story along these lines hit the television and print media in Australia and New Zealand recently, although I have heard of and investigated similar cases. This involved a woman who obtained literally thousands of dollars from men by simply offering her favors and the possibility of marriage. Of course, the guys who became involved with her never received what they thought was on offer, and when she was finally caught, their money had gone west with their hopes. I have to say that men are quite simply suckers for this type of scam because their little head rules their big head and their need to be attractive to women leaves them easy prey.

If you do end up meeting your Internet friend then protect not only your financial assets but also your emotional ones, because when someone is after you for financial gain they'll try emotional deception first. If in doubt, revert to the section "Beware of the wolf in sheep's clothing" and use the checklists to detect the cheaters from the good guys or girls.

### KEY POINTS

- Never give out personal financial details over the Web.
- Be careful as to how much personal information you release.
- Never send money to someone with a hard-luck story.
- If it's too good to be true it generally is.

## Predators on the Web

Generally, when people talk about betrayal they assume it takes place between two adults. However, with the Internet it is dangerous to assume anything.

My clients' 16-year-old daughter was spending every waking hour on the Web. It all started quite innocently on her part when she entered a chat room and began to chat with someone who, judging from his profile, was of a similar age.

They quickly struck up a friendship and little by little snippets of information came through suggesting he was a few years older than her (25 years older to be precise). But by this time she didn't care how old he was as they were firm friends. Then the mood of the conversations changed and he admitted to having strong feelings for her. He said this had never happened to him before and she was a very special person to arouse these feelings in him. (I deal with adults who fall for this crap, so is it any wonder that an impressionable 16-year-old girl was head over heels in love by this stage?)

The relationship moved from platonic to sexual—this had been his intention from the start. She was now saying and doing things a 16-year-old would not normally know about without a coach. It was at this point that her parents noticed a change in their once fun-loving and carefree daughter. She had become reclusive and had isolated herself from her usual group of friends at school. She found it impossible to relate to anyone and couldn't reveal her secret and sordid life with her older lover. Her schoolwork was suffering badly since she now spent most evenings and into the early hours talking on her cell phone or sending text messages to him.

This man was an evil predator who had spun his magic and she was totally enamored of him. He began to up the sexual ante and had her purchase a Web camera so he could watch her perform depraved acts. All this was being carried out without her ever having seen a picture of the man she was performing for, such is the power of these sexual predators.

It was no surprise to us to find this man was married with children and another on the way. He hadn't held down a job in years and it was his pregnant wife who was the breadwinner. They were in serious financial trouble and unable to pay their way. It was her parents who had to bail them out more often than they could afford.

His wife said he had a history of infidelity both on and off the Internet and that he had done this to his first wife with her ("If they do it with you they will do it to you"). The information we were able to give her came as a relief because she had known for years that their marriage was in serious trouble and with the support of her family this was enough to give her the strength to leave him.

Our clients were able to persuade their daughter into therapy but the road will be a long one for her. Unfortunately, when we went back on the Web, there he was, larger than life, working his magic on his next victim.

## KEY POINTS

- Keep a close watch on your children and make sure that you have free access to the computer area when teenagers (especially girls) are on the Web.
- Teenage girls are easy prey for predators.

# HOW TO HAVE
# AN AFFAIR

During the writing of this book I mentioned to a man that I was including a chapter on how to have an affair and he immediately commented that men wouldn't need to read this part of the book because they were the ones already having affairs. I replied: "No, you don't get it. They might be doing it but they need to read this chapter more than women because they are the ones who are getting caught." It took a few seconds but then I saw the light go on.

So in this section of the book I am going to endeavor to give you some guidelines on how to have an affair or perhaps keep you from getting caught. Whichever way you look at it, there are some fundamental rules that have to be followed in order to successfully carry on an affair.

Let me explain why I'm even devoting time to this subject and reassure you it's not as bad as you may think. When it comes to deceit, human nature is the cause of most people's downfall. If we were all emotionless creatures, there would be no need to concern ourselves with relationships and we could all be successful betrayers. In order to deceive, there are some very basic rules that must be followed religiously and even then they're not foolproof because there are other factors that come into play. One only has to look at the things people do that get them caught or exposed and work backwards from there, but that's a whole lot harder than it sounds.

I guess it's like someone living in poverty for most of their lives and then suddenly winning the lottery. It would be almost impossible not to do something that would alert people to their change in circumstances no matter how hard they may try. Any change, whether subtle or obvious, is what will first alert someone to the reality of a new situation. Therefore, it is crucial to act exactly as you did the day before meeting Mr. or Ms. Wonderful.

# The rules

## RULE 1: HONESTY

Honesty is an essential ingredient in conducting a successful affair. I know it sounds ridiculous talking about honesty in the same breath as deception but it is necessary.

How many times do married men pose as single men to attract women (usually single women)? This behavior is, quite simply, courting disaster. Single women are looking for a relationship and commitment whereas married men are acting indulgently and looking for self-gratification and nothing more. If you're married and posing as a single man it won't be too long before you blow your own cover because your lover is going to start asking questions. These questions will take one or more of the following forms:

"Why won't you stay the night?"

"Why can't we see each other over the weekend?"

"Why don't you give me your landline number instead of just your cell?"

"Why can't we go back to your house?"

"Where is your house?"

I don't need to tell you what's going to happen to you when your lover finds out she's been lied to—I'll leave that to your wife.

### RULE 2: DON'T ENTER INTO ANY SORT OF A LIAISON FROM A ONE-NIGHT STAND TO A LONG DRAWN-OUT AFFAIR WITH ANYONE IN YOUR WORKPLACE

Affairs are only that—they don't last and aren't meant to last. Remember only 5 percent of men leave their wives for a lover and when they do these relationships rarely last. Do you really want to end up having to face that person on a daily basis after an affair has turned sour? And is the potential risk to your other life really worth it? No office affair ever goes unnoticed by colleagues and therefore the chances of a disgruntled work colleague spilling the beans to your partner are high.

This rule also applies to your social circle, which may appear on the surface to offer the perfect opportunity by which to conduct an affair with someone already known to you and where the odd casual sighting may be easy to gloss over. This isn't the case, however, and it's virtually impossible to carry off because the friends who see you on a regular basis will notice even the subtlest of signs. Playing too close to home is a recipe for disaster.

### RULE 3: NEVER GET LOST IN THE HAZE

You need to be very clear about what you want from your affair and what you want from your marriage. Never under any circumstances should they merge. Your home life is exactly that, your life where you live with your wife and family. It is secure and comfortable, the practical stuff of day-to-day living. Your affair, on the other hand, is based on passion, sex and excitement. These are two very different worlds, therefore their identities must remain separate.

Don't fall into the trap of talking about how hard it is at home when in fact it isn't. I find men do this all too often when generally it's simply a throwaway line. Women take words so very literally that going down this path will be sure to backfire. Never discuss your home life with your lover just as you would never discuss your lover with your wife. It will only come back to haunt you.

## RULE 4: BUYING YOURSELF INTO A HOLE

I find most men can't help themselves—they just have to buy something special for the new woman in their life no matter how temporary she may be. It's an ego thing and a sure-fire way to fall flat on your face. This is twofold: firstly the effect on your lover is that she is going to wish she could meet someone as wonderful and generous as you to fall in love with permanently. Secondly she'll have ongoing expectations even if you started off the right way by stating the ground rules first. Actions such as giving gifts will send all that good work out the window. She'll start reading far more into it than you realize or ever intended. The wife, on the other hand, will find out, as they inevitably do.

I'm surprised at how many men pay for gifts for their lovers by credit card. I've lost count of the number of times a wife has found receipts for jewelry but, in typical female style, has nearly always given her husband the benefit of the doubt, thinking it must be a late birthday or anniversary present or just an "I love you" present. Alas, it never comes home.

I recall one client who knew her husband was having an affair. However, when she found the credit card statement from his recent overseas business trip she noticed he'd purchased an extremely expensive designer woman's coat and was rather excited because she couldn't imagine he would spend that kind of money on his floozy. As time went by and the coat never materialized she knew she was wrong. But, again in true female style, she lived in hope until one day in her husband's office she noticed a picture of his personal assistant on her desk and she was wearing the coat in question.

## RULE 5: DON'T SHIT IN YOUR OWN NEST

It astounds me how many affairs are carried out in the matrimonial home. I've heard a million times from my clients, "My husband would never bring anyone back here." Well, I'm sorry to be the bearer of bad news but the facts are the facts and I see it time and time again.

If you're going to shit in your own nest and you don't want to be discovered then you have to be very vigilant. If you're going to put some of your wife's possessions away before your lover arrives then make sure you put them back exactly where you found them and make sure you clean up after yourself—but not to the extent of Carol's husband. She'd been away for a week with the kids visiting family over the holidays while her husband stayed in the city because of work. When Carol got back the house was spotless and she was so impressed he'd gone to so much effort. It was about two or three days before she noticed a strange G-string in her underwear drawer. It was strange in that Carol's taste in underwear was always from a designer range and this item was definitely budget, but more importantly it wasn't even her size. She agonized over how it could have gotten there and by the time she rang me she'd conjured up every scenario imaginable.

It was later discovered that while Carol and the kids were away Ted was entertaining an escort in the house and the G-string belonged to her. It goes to show how little this husband knew about his wife's taste in underwear. If he'd taken more notice it would have cost him less grief.

Not only is stray underwear a problem, earrings, bracelets, lipsticks and other personal items left inadvertently or by design by your lover can give you away. Make sure if you find anything that doesn't belong to your wife that you dispose of it away from the house. Make sure you check inside pillowcases, the medicine cabinet, bedside drawers, and bathroom vanity areas and behind and under the bed.

Many an affair has been foiled by a nosy neighbor behind lace curtains because Neighborhood Watch is alive and well in the suburbs.

## RULE 6: THE LITTLE THINGS THAT MAKE US ALL UNIQUE

I mentioned earlier that other factors come into play when trying to keep an affair undetected. No matter how hard you try to do everything in your power to act as though nothing has changed and you are just the same today as you were yesterday, there are some things that are simply out of your control. So beware—your body can betray you, as Susan explains:

> I was fortunate (on reflection) in that I had already suffered two previous affairs so my intuitive antennae were already primed when the signals started falling into place. The final straw and actual confirmation that he was playing around was the most obvious one—sex! We had become in a lot of ways more like brother and sister and our sex life had become something I instigated as a

form of love and affection. If he hadn't had sex for a couple of weeks he had a habit of farting when he ejaculated but if we had sex frequently this didn't occur. All of a sudden I noticed his farting had ceased no matter how long the intervals between us having sex. That's when I knew for certain.

So, essentially, even if Susan hadn't had the previous betrayals to hasten her awareness that John was playing around, his body would one day have given him up to his fate. You may not be aware of your idiosyncrasies, but your partner will be.

## RULE 7: THERE'S NO SUCH THING AS A SECRET WHEN TWO PEOPLE KNOW

I'm sure you've all heard the saying "Loose lips sink ships." In other words the only people who need to know about your affair are the two of you.

Men are prone to letting their egos get in the way and often when under the influence of alcohol will brag to their buddies about their most recent conquest. Women, when meeting friends for lunch, have a permanent grin and that faraway look in their eyes, which leads to questions they don't want to answer but often do.

Human nature is a curious thing and jealousy is a destructive emotion. Although they may be your friends your happiness can create more problems than you bargained for. It only takes a few words for problems to occur and your ship to go down, so resist the temptation to share your affair with anyone.

## RULE 8: PAPER TRAIL

The computer can be your worst enemy so ensure you don't communicate with your lover from your home computer. Even if you think you've deleted all the e-mail evidence a forensic computer expert will be able to retrieve it without any problems whatsoever.

Don't password-protect the home computer. One of the most important rules is: "If you have nothing to hide you hide nothing." The most significant pointer to you having something to hide is a password to the home computer that only you know.

Don't think that just because you tossed out your cell phone bills you're in the clear. If you're asked to prove your trustworthiness by allowing your wife to view your phone records, saying you can't find them won't cut the mustard. Records are kept for seven years and a simple phone call to your telephone company will reveal all.

## RULE 9: CHOOSE YOUR LOVER CAREFULLY

The next fundamental strategy is your choice of lover and that choice is critical to the success or failure of an impending affair—so choose your lover wisely. This is another potential area for disaster, so make sure the person you choose is emotionally mature, emotionally stable and understands fully that an affair means, fun, excitement, no strings, no commitment, no future together—just sex. The rules need to be worked out before you embark on a physical relationship. It must be made clear you're going to stay married and therefore you need acknowledgment from your potential lover that these conditions are acceptable and understood.

## RULE 10: NEVER EVER HAVE UNPROTECTED SEX

I cannot believe the naivety of people when it comes to STDs and unwanted pregnancies. These can certainly be some of the most obvious giveaways. Just because he's had a vasectomy, or she's on the pill or has had a tubal ligation or hysterectomy, don't assume that everything is safe; these only stop babies, not diseases. Never discount your lover's partner. There are many men who believe that if their lover is married she doesn't pose a risk but who's to say what her husband's been up to?

The number of one-night stands that end in pregnancy is higher than you would imagine. The same goes for how many of my clients find out about an affair only after contracting an STD. Therefore protection is literally vital to survival.

## RULE 11: MAKE CALLS ON YOUR CELL PHONE AT YOUR PERIL

What would we do without our cell phones? Well, let me tell you that the worst thing any self-respecting cheater can do is use their personal or company cell phone to conduct an affair. Modern cells offer the wife or partner numerous ways in which to trace calls or text messages without having phone bills to check. Just think of all the opportunities your partner has to check your phone for calls received or made: when you're in the shower, mowing the lawn or any time you're asleep. Of course you can always delete all messages and numbers before you get home, put a PIN number on it, leave it locked in the car or sleep with it but any or all of these will cause suspicion—so don't.

The solution to this predicament is to buy a prepaid phone and keep it somewhere private. Don't buy the prepaid phone with any form of money card. It is wise to scrape together some cash that can't be traced to a transaction that will appear on a statement. When you buy prepaid, don't do it with your credit card or debit card as these come up on statements. Always use cash, and withdraw small denominations so large sums don't show up on your statements.

Do remember that no system is foolproof and it will take just the smallest slip (which is all we need) for your house of cards (because that's what affairs are) to come crashing down.

## RULE 12: KEEP YOUR THOUGHTS OFF PAPER

When men betray they tend to put their thoughts on paper, more often than women. These thoughts often weigh up the pros and cons of the wife and lover and are written on random pieces of paper and left in a briefcase or office drawer just waiting for a suspicious wife to find. In a number of cases this has been the man's downfall and has led to him being exposed. It also provides strong ammunition for the wife to use in the face of denial.

## RULE 13: THE EXIT PLAN

This is where all your careful planning should pay off. In all affairs there comes a time when it's over. The reason isn't really important, there will be many: maybe the thrill of the chase has worn off or the benefits don't exceed the deceit. Whatever the reason the time from now on is crucial to your survival. If you have conducted yourself as I have advised and haven't made outrageous promises that haven't been fulfilled, have been honest with your lover about your expectations then there is a chance (however slim) that you may survive this affair.

However, we're only human and these rules cover the most important aspects of human frailty; breaking just one of these will lead to your downfall. I feel this needs to be said because some of you will no doubt try and hold me personally responsible for people flying off in all directions and having affairs. One can lead a horse to water but one can't make it drink—and the same is true here.

I've often said that those who choose to betray their partners have a behavioral weakness, arrogance and an "I don't give a shit" kind of attitude. You are either monogamous or you're not. However, one can never lose sight of the fact that it all boils down to choice.

The very reason people have affairs is that they consciously choose to do so. No one forces them. So many people use the excuse that it "just happened," but it doesn't just happen. Your clothes don't fall off while you're walking down the street.

Having an affair is something you have to plan and construct and the very reason you skulk around corners trying not to get caught is because you know it's wrong, but the truth of the matter is that you don't give a shit. So don't try the oldest trick in the book by transferring the blame onto me for bringing this out into the open; take responsibility for your actions and remember that for every action there is a reaction.

## Mistresses beware

If he's doing it with you he may well be doing it to you. To all mistresses out there, just bear with me for a while. If you're single and have considered the pros and cons of this liaison and you have absolutely no expectations and are under no illusions (because this is purely a physical attraction and once the spark goes so will you, without a backward glance), then maybe you will enjoy your fling with your married lover. But if you're looking for something more and want a future with this man and you're willing to give your heart to him, then you need to tread very carefully. Just stop for a moment and think of his wife. He's probably told you they've been having problems for some time and they may not even sleep together anymore and there you are like a breath of fresh air that has entered his life. Let's assume his wife finds out about you because sooner or later she will. She's devastated because she had no idea they were having problems and as for sleeping in separate rooms—I don't think so. Can you imagine her shock? Well, try, because that's exactly how you will feel in due course. As sure as the day is long, if you stay with this man he will do exactly the same to you.

You need to take a reality check and carefully consider your lover, this married man who's been lying to his wife for as long as you've been involved with him. Why do you believe he's telling you the truth? Just because he says he is? If his life is so bad at home (with no sex, sleeping in the spare room, no communication apart from the occasional argument) then why does he still stay there? I'll tell you why, because it's not that bad or it's not bad at all but he paints a picture for you and for himself that allows you both to feel these circumstances are valid reasons for betraying his wife.

What if he gave you the following explanation? "Hi, sweetheart, I'm a prick of a guy, I love my wife, I don't want to leave my comfortable home or split my wealth, I'm just a greedy bastard, I don't want to have sex with just one woman so don't think I'm going to fall in love with you. A guy like me has to do what he wants, when he wants." Now, would you have an affair with this guy? I think not but if you do, you need to first acknowledge that this is who he really is.

You actually have no idea whether he has had serial dalliances elsewhere during your time with him. Your lover is a liar so stop being naive and remember: "If he does it with you the chances are he will do it to you."

# A WORD TO THE GUYS

What is it with you guys? Is it the lack of emotional maturity that has you measuring your manliness by the number of women you've had sex with? Or does it have something to do with low self-esteem and a lack of confidence? I know it's perceived that members of the fairer sex are the ones needing constant attention but men are like sponges when it comes to flattery. I think it's true to say that men believe in fairytales more than women. They still believe girls are made from "sugar and spice and everything nice." Women are far more devious than men believe or ever give them credit for. Of course there are wonderful, warm, loving, caring women out there looking for Mr. Wonderful. However, that's "Mr. Single Wonderful," not "Mr. Married with Kids."

The women that don't fit that category come with varying degrees of danger attached. Some are demanding, controlling, manipulative, greedy, mercenary and sheer ruthless—but with enough sugar coating to disguise the fact. Then there are the ones who appear to be coy, feeble, vulnerable and helpless, the "I've never had a good relationship with anyone before until you came along" kinda gal and this is the one who appeals to the "knight in shining armor" kinda guy. Finally, there are the ones who are a little more obvious and come with drinking problems, are physically and verbally abusive and can be irrational and extremely volatile and yet because these women will say they love you, you can't possibly reject them. She wants you. She really wants you!

Why is it men feel that if the bus stops here they have to get on, and without thinking of the consequences? The male need for female approval is a major concern and the key to avoiding getting on the wrong bus, or any bus if you're married, is to ask yourself why you're at the bus stop in the first place. What do you want? What do you need? And what do you already have? A truly confidant man already knows how incredibly special and unique he is. That doesn't mean he can't enjoy a compliment, it just means that when some stunning female pays him some attention he's emotionally mature enough to acknowledge it without his ego getting in the way and jeopardizing everything he has.

## For all those philanderers out there

What I find so incredible about this whole issue of infidelity is that there's a bunch of you out there who meet, find attractive and finally fall in love with women, and then without any regard go about making their lives miserable.

The two most overused excuses by men in defense of their infidelity are either: *She was just someone I could talk to because we were having problems* or *I just need to move out for a few months so I can sort myself out.*

Yeah, right, that makes a whole lot of sense. It's really helpful to rebuild your relationship with your wife by having sex with someone else and it makes even more sense to try and fix your relationship when you've removed yourself from it. And then you honestly wonder why you can't seem to get that old level of intimacy back and those feelings of love. You'll say: "How can I when this woman is always on my case? She's prying into my every move and constantly rehashing the past at every opportunity."

What will it take before you guys get it? Remaining faithful is all that's required and that means being devoted, dependable, reliable, constant and truthful. How hard is that? There is no other magic ingredient to a successful happy relationship full of fun, love and passion. When a woman knows in her heart that she's the one, the only one, and if she feels she can fully trust her man then the flames of passion burn bright. And boys, you don't know what you're missing because it's a fact that women become more sexual and passionate as the years go by. Surely you haven't forgotten how fantastic your life together was in the beginning? That's because you made a promise to be faithful and she believed you but once you breached that promise you waived your rights. The chances of getting back what you had are slight at best and non-existent if you ever repeat the offense.

For all those philanderers out there who truly want to make their relationship work: the answer doesn't lie in how successful you perceive yourself to be; how others see you; how financially well off you are; how intelligent you are or what education you have; but has everything to do with your level of emotional maturity and integrity. The majority of my clients' husbands are in their late thirties to fifties but display the emotional maturity of a five-year-old—"I want what I want when I want it and I want it now."

There is nothing more unattractive to a woman than an emotionally immature man. In fact, real men don't behave in this manner. If you know in your heart that you can't handle temptation without wanting to take it one step further (and this type of behavior doesn't just sneak up on you overnight; you know as well as I do that you've been like this all your adult life) then what you need to do is be man enough to stand up and take responsibility. Either leave or clean up your act once and for all. You don't have the right to ruin the lives of those around you, i.e., your wife and family.

I have a simple question to ask. If you look at all your indiscretions (probably meaningless ones in your mind) would you have done any of them with your wife standing next to you? You know the answer as well as I do, so don't try to minimize the gravity of your immaturity in the choices you have made.

Then there's the message you're sending to your children, because behavior like this is usually learned. Is this how you would want your sons to behave and would you want a man who treats women with the same disrespect as you do to marry your daughter? If not, think about the message you're sending.

Let me tell you something that I absolutely know for sure—how to measure your success as a man. It's when your words and actions match. It's when you have the integrity to do the right thing when no one else is watching. If you take nothing else from the book, let it be this.

The ground rules to an honest and committed relationship are simple: the proof is in the evidence. She's not interested in what you say, she's only interested in what you're going to do. This means no secrecy and no lies. If you've had your cell phone bill, your credit card accounts and your bank statements moved from home to your office, send them back home again. The only way to prove you have nothing to hide is by hiding nothing. Leave your briefcase unlocked, take the PIN number off your phone, remove the password from the computer—you have to be an open book and become predictable. This is the only way you'll have any hope of retrieving your relationship. If you can't or won't do these things then she'll never ever be able to get over your infidelity and I mean never. The choice is yours.

# Let's talk about control

I know a lot of you guys don't see yourselves as control freaks but many of you are, whether you're willing to admit it or not. There's no need for the wife to be bothered with the mundane matter of money, right? Wrong. This isn't 1950, when it was accepted that the man handled the finances and the little wife kept home and dared not question her husband. Women today do want a say in the family finances. After all, it's supposed to be an equal partnership you've entered into. If you keep investments, stocks, bank accounts, trusts and mortgages to yourself and are under the illusion that you can do what you want with the joint assets (and that's what they are) then that is called control.

Too often I come across women who are the wives or partners of men like you. Men who control the family finances purely and simply to fund their infidelities and then live under the illusion that as long as their wives are well taken care of they'll have no grounds for complaint.

You might think this will give you free rein but let me tell you that when you continue to control in this way, in the long run it will effectively work against you. Your wife didn't enter into a relationship to go backwards, but under this amount of control that is exactly what she's doing. Our parents controlled us for our own good but then we matured and in most cases left that control and went out on our own. Think about it in this way: do you want to be seen by your wife as her father? Too much of this and she's going to leave your control or maybe turn the tables on you.

You can try and justify to yourself that this is for her own good but that's bullshit. If it was for her own good, why all the secrecy? We both know the reason for that: "When you've got nothing to hide you hide nothing."

If you are spending joint funds on another woman or women then stop and think, whose money is it? Half of it belongs to your wife or partner and you can bet all the tea in China that if she knew what you were doing with it then it wouldn't be happening. The ultimate test is the next time you are siphoning off funds or setting up another trust in which your spouse or partner isn't involved. Would you do it if she knew what the consequences were for her long-term future?

The biggest catalyst for a wife or partner to seek legal advice isn't financial betrayal but emotional betrayal and the uncovering of one leads more often than not to the uncovering of the other, so keep in mind that the day of reckoning is never far away.

# The link between porn and infidelity

I'm going to share with you something I absolutely know for sure. How I know this is purely and simply by the overwhelming amount of evidence I've had over the years. Many of the women I work for (your wives, girlfriends or partners) seek my advice because they think there must be something wrong with them sexually. Some are being pressured into sexual situations not to their liking while others find themselves living in sexless relationships. This is because you're so caught up in playing out your fantasies and visiting prostitutes that you lose the ability to function in the real world with real women, i.e., your wives, girlfriends or partners.

As I've said, this makes it impossible for your wives, girlfriends or partners to live up to your fantasies, so over time you turn off from what's real and live with what's not.

These women are torn between their love for you and wanting to please you, and their own sense of self-preservation. The reason they feel this way is because they're not comfortable with some of your sexual desires and demands.

Let's make something perfectly clear from the start: I'm no prude. If I were I wouldn't have lasted five minutes in this job because there are times where it feels like I am literally working in the sex industry. The evidence shows a common thread that runs through certain dysfunctional relationships— pornography and infidelity. The two go hand in hand.

I've lost count of the complaints I hear from women who tell me they've gone along with sexual activities because of the pressure brought to bear by you. They wouldn't normally consider these activities but they do so in order to fulfill your fantasies and desires, only to feel sick, humiliated and degraded. Often this is an attempt on their part to try to be more accommodating so you don't stray again. They don't want you to come down on them with the old guilt trip: "Well, honey, if you would only be more sexually adventurous I wouldn't need to go looking for it." (Oh, please. Get a grip!) However, there are lots of women who will try almost anything to keep their man, no matter how humiliating. When on the other hand they refuse to participate, they're made to feel unloving and inadequate as women.

The activities you want them to participate in range from group sex to watching you have sex with both women and men or wanting to watch your wife have sex with another woman. You'll have come up with various reasons for wanting this behavior, the biggest crock being how it will bring the two of you closer together. Having disconnected sex for sexual gratification alone doesn't enhance a loving intimate relationship, especially when it's performed under duress.

You guys are incredibly transparent, not only to me but to the women in your lives. However, they're afraid or unsure how to confront this issue and what I usually tell them is this: it's like someone asking you to do something that isn't sexual or illegal but wrong in your eyes. You have every right to decline. It is your right to live the life you want and to which you are entitled. It has nothing to do with what anyone else says is normal but it has everything to do with what you feel is right. And that's what counts.

Men who put the pressure on and try to manipulate and control through sex are usually inadequate, incapable of true emotional intimacy and trust. The same goes for guys who frequent prostitutes and spend hours in porn sites and chat rooms on the Internet. This is escapism, a quick fix for an ongoing problem. Guys who participate in these forms of sexual gratification feel fantastic, acceptable and masculine without ever earning or deserving it. But it never ends there and that's where I come in.

So as much as you try to justify it—it's harmless fun or you're only looking—when will you get the message that women don't want men who are constantly looking at, wanting or having other women?

## What it is that women want

Let me tell you what they're really looking for: a man who is confident in himself and desires only one woman—THEM!

The more you show the woman in your life that you desire variety and she's just not enough woman for a man like you, the further you push her out of your heart. Thank God there are real men out there, men who have got it. They have everything you want and crave. They have variety and excitement, fantastic fulfilling, mind-blowing sex combined with passion, admiration, love, respect and commitment—and all with just one woman.

"My God, how can that be possible?" you ask. Well, firstly they grew up and learned a few simple rights from wrongs. They developed emotional maturity instead of being

emotional cowards. They aren't on a quest for external fulfillment because they've realized that self-worth is far more
important than an over-inflated ego (the downfall of many a
man). They're happy in the knowledge that actions speak
louder than words. But more importantly they learned long
ago that you get out of your relationship what you put in and
believe me when I say there is nothing more desirable and
sexy to a healthy and intelligent woman than an emotionally
mature, confident man of integrity.

# WHEN YOU LIVE
# WITH A LIAR

When you live with a liar there are certain behavioral traits you may encounter, most significantly the will to deceive. Whether the lie is blatant or a lie by omission the intention is the same. It is a conscious and deliberate act to conceal or misrepresent the truth to keep you from knowing the facts.

Lying in a relationship will erode it over time and there is nothing more destructive to your health and well-being than living with a liar. There are so many ways in which people can lie and those men who lie will try to rationalize, minimize and justify their behavior when caught. They may offer up one or many of the following excuses:

- I had good reason.
- I didn't want to hurt you.
- I didn't mean to.
- It just happened.
- I was drunk.

Women on the other hand will often rationalize, minimize and justify their partners' lying to avoid dealing with the truth. This may take any of the following forms:

- Well, he's only human after all.
- I know he didn't want to hurt me.
- It's probably my fault; I've put on weight.

Then there is the transferring of guilt by the liar. He may say something like:

- You make me feel like you don't care anymore.
- Oh, well, you accused me of having an affair so I thought I might as well have one.
- If only you'd have looked after yourself more it wouldn't have happened.

So what do women do? They take the guilt on board and start believing they've driven their husband into the arms of another woman because they're too fat, too thin, too tall, too short, too old, not exciting enough—the list is endless. Men will always try to get themselves off the hook by making it their partners' fault. Don't get caught up in the blame game. Remember there is no excuse for his lying to you. You can't make him lie to you—lying was his choice and his decision.

The artful dodger is the guy who appears to be going to take responsibility for his actions but then in mid-flight changes gear and tries shifting the blame on to the other woman.

It all started with a lipstick stain on a pristine white business shirt. When Pete arrived home the first thing his wife noticed was the lipstick stain on the inside of his shirt collar. Pete had to come clean and confess all, but instead of owning responsibility he made it out to be the woman's fault. He explained to his wife that when he'd returned to the office to pick up some papers one of the women was just about to leave and they got to chatting. "Then out of the blue she took off her blouse and unbuttoned my shirt and took it off and started kissing me. She was making all the moves but nothing happened. I wasn't even attracted to her. I've said I'm sorry. What more do you want?"

If your husband has betrayed you and has been backed into a corner then he's probably had to acknowledge to you that he's cheated on you. This acknowledgment comes complete with protestations such as: "I'm sorry, it will never happen again," or "I'll prove to you that you can trust me," and he will usually feel after such an apology that he's vindicated and you should give him credit for his confession.

Jack was a master at lying and cheating and apologizing and confessing but when caught he was never able to deliver on any of his promises. When Jack had made an apology, in his mind the matter was closed.

Two weeks after his latest infidelity and, on being caught, his subsequent confession, Jack and his wife were watching a television program in which the husband was caught cheating on his wife. Jack looked across at his wife and there were tears in her eyes because any reminder of her own situation was an emotional torment and after only two weeks her wounds were fresh. Jack asked her, "What's the matter with you?"

She replied, "I'll give you three guesses," to which Jack said, "Oh, no, not that again. I thought you were over it."

Jack's wife asked me what she should do about his attitude and this is what I told her. "This isn't about what Jack says. It's about what Jack needs to do and what is non-negotiable in your relationship in order to make progress. Your role is to have a list of requirements and not to back down no matter how heartfelt his words may be. This is about actions. It's about Jack taking responsibility and actively working on changing his behavior so that in the future he makes healthy choices."

When a grown man who's never shed a tear in his life suddenly bursts into tears when confronted with his lies, beware, because he may very well be playing on your sympathies. Watch out for phrases such as:

- I feel so bad about this.
- OK, so I lied but I didn't kill anyone.
- You know I love you and would do anything for you.
- My actions make me so depressed I feel like killing myself.

These pathetic responses need dealing with in a firm way. Let him know quite clearly you are aware he's upset but you've been more than upset by his lies, and if he doesn't respond to your needs there can be no way forward.

# Danger! Danger!

This is the worst man you may have the misfortune to encounter. He is dangerous, blatant, single-minded, self-centered, egotistical and extremely persuasive. There aren't enough words to describe a man like this other than to say he comes across as charming, understanding, sensitive, romantic, exciting and is often a good lover but there is a vital part of him missing. He is incapable of love—feeling it or giving it. Although he may say "I love you," even this is a lie because his actions towards you will be anything but loving. He simply doesn't have the components required and there is simply nothing you can do to change this man.

He is incapable of any depth of feeling because he is a sociopath and through my work I've met a number of them. These men do the most damage and the dreadful reality is that no amount of counseling and therapy will have any effect and I'm sure many psychologists will agree with me on this one. It's a waste of time punishing a sociopath; they never learn from experience, as there is always another victim around the corner. There may be windows of hope when he appears to see the error of his ways but there's nothing anyone can do to prevent this man from reverting to the way he was.

Alice met a sociopath and four years later she still bears the scars. Charles was a highly respected man among his peers, but then no one really knew much about Charles's private life and certainly not his dark side. Alice met Charles at a conference they were attending. He was charming and attentive and this led to an intense few days together. Alice was totally swept off her feet. She couldn't believe she'd met a man who was so sensitive, listened to what she had to say and certainly looked the part. But Charles was playing a role and this behavior had nothing to do with who Charles really was. In fact, Charles didn't know who the real Charles was.

The sociopath is like a chameleon; they change their persona to suit the environment and situation. Charles had worked his charm and in a very short time had convinced Alice to leave her husband and children. Alice moved into a house and waited for Charles to leave his wife and join her as promised. But Charles had no intention of living with Alice or Christine or Janet, all of whom were waiting for him. Two of these women confronted his wife but so plausible was his story (to his wife) she totally believed him and is still with him today. All three women are trying to piece together their broken lives.

The best way to get over a romantic encounter with a sociopath is to make an appointment with a psychologist to gain an understanding of how a sociopath operates. This will be the first step in moving forward.

# WOMEN WHO LEAVE

Women who stay in abusive and dysfunctional relationships and marriages are well represented in this book, as are the reasons they stay. Take, for example, the reaction you get when confronting a man about the affair he's been having with his personal assistant at work. You give him an ultimatum: either she goes or you go. Then listen to the barrage of reasons he gives as to why this can't happen. Now ask yourself why you stay and listen to all those reasons. You'll find that what you're both doing is giving lists of excuses. If you were to be honest with yourself you would see that standing in your way is self-doubt, discomfort and fear. But if you were to be true to yourself you would know that all of these things could be worked on and overcome.

So what about the women who leave these relationships behind? Where do they fit into the scheme of things and what type of woman is it that can make this most difficult of choices? I've already pointed out that women perceive it easier to stay than leave (my own files back this up) and so I know it takes great courage and self-respect.

It isn't so clear just what type of woman is capable of making such a difficult choice because when such a decision is made, it is often made by the woman who, on first meeting, would seem the most unlikely to take such action.

If I had to nail it down then I would say that these women all have great inner strength and a desire first and foremost to look after themselves and in doing so, their future and that of any children. In the wild a lioness feeds herself first so she will have the strength to hunt again and in turn feed her cubs so they can grow and survive to make the pride stronger. A modern analogy is when an aircrew gives instructions on the use of oxygen masks. Adults traveling with young children are instructed to fit their own oxygen masks first before attending to any children. Women who decide to leave aren't selfish individuals but women who know that if they don't do it for themselves then their lives and those of their children will suffer in the long term.

In this section I'm going to describe three such courageous women in the hopes that those of you who think it's easier to stay will take heart and hope from their experiences and realize that in making these choices, you can, like them, come out on top.

## Mercedes, Mary and Bernice

Although all three women have been equally courageous I'm going to begin by focusing on Mercedes, because on first meeting she seemed the most unlikely to take such a step—considering her circumstances. How wrong could I have been?

Mercedes was 17 when she met Edgar, a construction worker and pastor at her church. With limited education and totally unworldly, Mercedes was fair game for Edgar, 18 years her senior and already into his second marriage. Edgar set about snaring the innocent Mercedes, which he did, and having done so dumped wife number two for a new life with Mercedes. They quickly had two children and Mercedes became the dutiful wife and mother, totally controlled by Edgar. Whatever Edgar wanted, Mercedes had to provide and it became clear during our meetings that Mercedes saw deviant sexual practices as normal because that was all she knew. God-fearing Edgar would, on the surface, be seen as a "family man," a "man's man," who worked long hours in the construction industry but this couldn't be further from the truth because the real Edgar had a number of secrets.

After more than ten years of marriage the light went on and Mercedes began to question her life with Edgar. Mercedes called me and asked questions about what was acceptable in a marriage. I think I left her with more questions than answers and our association went on from there.

It was clear she had serious issues to overcome but what impressed me most about this young woman was that with no ready source of money or emotional backing she was absolutely adamant that no one was going to make a fool of her. From the time I started working with her to the moment of truth, her inner strength and belief in herself never wavered. Her lack of financial independence and a tight budget should have been a hurdle but her tenacity came to the fore. She scrimped and scraped money together because she was sure Edgar was being unfaithful. But who with was the burning question.

What we uncovered was a secret life in that he was bisexual and always had been, yet could never come out, partly because the construction industry was extremely macho. However, on speaking to his former wives (and there were three, not two) it became clear they had all found themselves in Mercedes' situation.

Armed with this information Mercedes set about carrying out her "exit plan" with military precision, not letting Edgar know she was aware of his secret until she had departed. Despite the deep sense of betrayal Mercedes acted with dignity in that she never revealed to anyone what she had uncovered, and to this day Edgar's reputation remains intact. I think of Mercedes often when I am dealing with many of my clients. They make excuses and continue to live in the emotional hell they have created while Mercedes lives in emotional peace.

Mary's story is another example of a woman taking stock of her life and choosing to leave for a life free of emotional turmoil and stress—and doing so while coping with a pregnancy.

Mary and Dan married young and in 16 years of marriage had focused on building up their individual businesses and a portfolio of property. Dan had always wanted a family, more so than Mary, and time was ticking by, so before the biological clock stopped they decided to try for a baby. After 18 months of trying they were both ecstatic when Mary discovered she was pregnant with twins. However, Mary was so preoccupied with the effects of the early stages of a multiple pregnancy that she missed some vital warning signs. Dan was acting out of character.

Up to this point Dan had been the model husband, but at this critical time of need for comfort and support Dan seemed remote and detached. Mary found this behavior from the man she had known for 16 years so out of keeping with his desire to have a family that she began to wonder what was going on. Mary was completely exhausted with the constant throwing up caused by her pregnancy so her mother suggested that since Dan was at work all day she should come and stay with her until this period was over. Mary was glad to have the rest and stayed for ten days.

On her return, feeling much fitter and stronger, she noticed right away that all her personal items had been put on the floor of the wardrobe, including her pregnancy books. She asked Dan why this was and he told her he'd been cleaning the house before her return and had forgotten to put them back.

This again was totally out of character as Dan had never cleaned the house in 16 years of marriage, but once again she took this to be his way of helping with the pregnancy.

Dan always had his phone close by but had now taken to carrying it with him even when taking out the trash. Then one evening they decided to go out for dinner. They found a parking space right outside the restaurant entrance, which was perfect for Mary since she was now quite large and found walking any distance uncomfortable. They went inside and Mary went to use the bathroom. On her return to the table Dan said he had to move the car, which, considering where they'd parked it some five minutes ago, was totally crazy. Dan returned and fudged his answers as to why he'd needed to move the vehicle. Some ten minutes later he also needed to use the bathroom and for once left his phone on the table. Mary was by now sure something was going on and used the memory to show the last phone number, which she wrote down.

When Mary told me the story thus far I was fairly convinced Dan was up to no good. Having called the number Mary had written down and found it belonged to a girl at his office, about whom he'd made some derogatory remarks, I knew then that we were on the right track. I suggested to Mary that she should return to her mother for a few days and we would find the answers to her dilemma.

We set up surveillance down the road from Mary's home. Within five minutes of Mary having arrived at her mother's, a car was pulling up outside Mary's home and a young woman, who was later revealed as the woman Dan phoned from outside the restaurant, entered the house by a side gate. These visits were a regular occurrence during Mary's three-day stay at her mother's. Our investigations revealed this woman was also married and the relationship between her and Dan had been going on for a number of years.

Dan denied and denied, and even faced with our report continued to deny, making up every excuse imaginable for her being there. The last straw was when Dan gave as one of the reasons for the woman being there that she needed somewhere to deposit a wine bottle and was looking for a recycling bin. The fact that she had her own recycling bin at home and had passed two recycling plants on her 15-mile journey across town didn't register with Dan and he was amazed that Mary would challenge his explanation.

Despite her condition and the immense stress of the situation Mary remained steadfast and calm, and she knew where her boundaries lay. Mary now has a son and daughter and juggles motherhood and work with the same sense of calmness with which she handled the predicament she found herself in. I'll leave the last words to her.

> This has been the hardest time of my life. I don't think I'll ever get over how this man could blatantly lie to me and deny any wrongdoing. I cannot even imagine what I must have done to deserve this but when I look at my children I know I wouldn't change a thing. There are times when I feel cheated because my husband wasn't there for me at the birth and he isn't there for me now. He has only seen his children once in 12 months, although it all fades into insignificance when I think back to what it was like agonizing over his every move and analyzing everything that he said. At least I'm a totally-free-and-getting-happier-by-the-day spirit. How anyone can raise children and do themselves justice when your life and thoughts are filled with such destruction is beyond me.

The third of our women is Bernice, a full-on mother of four teenaged boys, and if ever there was a reason to stay then

Bernice had it in abundance. She and Andrew owned a very successful business, had an affluent lifestyle in a highly sought after residential area and a wide circle of family and friends.

While returning from the weekly grocery shopping Bernice noticed Andrew's new fire-engine-red Jaguar close to home at a time when he was supposed to be at a meeting at his office. By the time she'd turned around, his car had disappeared and although she searched the area there was no sign of the vehicle. When Andrew arrived home he made no mention of being in the area and openly talked about his meeting so she gave him the benefit of the doubt.

Over the next few weeks she couldn't shake a nagging feeling that something just wasn't quite right, because Andrew had been a little distant for some months, so she decided to check the phone records. What stood out were numerous phone calls on a daily basis to a cell number, which belonged to the wife of one of their friends. Armed with this information she confronted him, in true female style, and to her surprise he didn't deny the calls, saying he was helping her with problems she was having in her marriage. Bernice couldn't understand why this woman hadn't mentioned the problems she was having since they'd had coffee the previous week and had, as usual, covered a wide range of topics.

Bernice was on red alert and took a trip to the area where she'd seen the Jaguar but still couldn't understand what reason he would have to be there because the woman in question didn't live in that area. After a fruitless search Bernice called me and I recommended we search property registers. And what do you know? Andrew owned a property in the area she'd been searching, but the reason she couldn't find the vehicle was that the property was down a long driveway with internal garaging and surrounded by bushes—making it the perfect setting for a love nest.

Bernice was blown away and it took some time for her to comprehend the scale of deceit. Although she questioned Andrew many times he wouldn't admit to having an affair and said he'd bought the property as an investment for them and was going to tell her (but WHEN—considering he'd owned it for three years and in his name only?).

Armed with this information Bernice sought legal advice and eventually separated from Andrew, explaining to me that there was no way she was going to allow her sons to see that this was how a man treats a woman.

This woman showed true self-respect and faced her fears head on because she had no concrete evidence of physical betrayal, which most women seem to feel they need but still do nothing with.

About one year later I had a call from Bernice, who asked me to sit down because I wasn't going to believe what she had to tell me. Her eldest son's best friend had a sister who they'd recently found out was moonlighting as an escort to help her through college. She'd confided in her brother that Bernice's husband was one of her best paying clients and had been for more than three years. She went on to say she'd been able to walk from her home to his place and described the secret hideaway.

For Bernice this information was like the icing on the cake. Her gut instinct had been 100 percent accurate. Bernice reiterated there was no way her boys were going to grow up learning how to treat a woman from their father. She concluded that Andrew would always be their father and was a good dad—just a lousy husband.

All of these women made decisions based on evidence that these men couldn't be believed or trusted again. I'm often asked what should someone do—stay or leave—but I can't answer that because it's such an individual choice. Some people can survive living with infidelity and some can't. There is no specific timetable for leaving but it's probably fair to say there is more fear attached to thinking about ending a relationship than actually doing it. If the time is ever right it's only after you can say with a clear conscience that you've done everything in your power to try and salvage your relationship. Sometimes it feels as though something has shifted inside you and then you know that this is what you need to do in order for your life to go forward. However, you don't want to leave when you're still resentful and angry because these are the emotions you should have worked through before you go. If you don't you'll end up anxious and dissatisfied that you've made the wrong choice and this will hold you in the past, feeling regretful for what you've lost, when in fact you'll only be feeling sorry for what you thought you had.

## KEY POINTS

- All these women had a clear definition of their boundaries.
- All made the decision to leave based on evidence that their husbands couldn't be trusted again.
- Each had true self-respect.

### GRIEF

Betrayal causes a grief that rocks you to the very core of your foundations. It affects every aspect of your life and you literally feel paralyzed with the pain. During the course of your life you're likely to encounter many hurts but your partner's betrayal may enrage and hurt you like nothing else has.

Many of my clients who have experienced the death of a loved one actually described the grief of their husband's betrayal as harder to deal with because as devastating as death is, we all know it's final. We may experience anger and hurt at that person leaving us but betrayal is premeditated; someone doesn't deliberately set out to hurt you by dying. They don't plan their death. In other words, they have no intent to hurt you, unlike an unfaithful partner.

If your husband does finally leave you for another woman then it's not just the hurt that you experience but the insult to your dignity and intelligence, together with a deep feeling of loss for what you thought you had (i.e., love, trust and stability). And if all that isn't hard enough to come to terms with, you then have to start to build a new life for yourself at an age where you should be enjoying the fruits of the years spent together building a future. This hurt is compounded when the other woman is seen enjoying the lifestyle and position you've spent years working towards.

Ella and Barry have been married for 28 years and for most of their married life they had run a very successful business together. Ella phoned me because she'd noticed Barry was taking a more than keen interest in one of the female staff. Ella explains:

> This is not the first time he's done this and I can't ignore it anymore. I'm going crazy and obsessing about everything. I hit rock bottom the other day. I normally go through his clothing, checking his shirts, looking in trouser pockets for receipts ... I'm not even sure what I'm looking for although I'm probably looking for a hotel receipt (but I can't imagine where he takes her because he's so tight with money), but now I'm checking his underwear and that's so humiliating. I've got to stop and deal with this because it's taking over my life.

Ella was right. He wasn't paying for a hotel; he was taking her to a park a short distance from work. The deed was all over and done with in a matter of minutes, then he would drop her back at her car and go on and have lunch with some male friends.

Ella was disgusted by her husband's behavior, but because Barry was scheduled to go overseas for a conference she decided to use that time to come to terms with her decision. Barry had only been away for four days when I heard from Ella. She told me he'd suffered a serious heart attack and died. Ella was in terrible pain for the loss of the man she still loved but much greater was the anger she felt for not having had the opportunity to confront him and gain acknowledgment from him for all the hurt and suffering he'd caused her throughout their marriage. Because she'd never confided in anyone, no one knew the extent of the emotional turmoil this woman was going through, but she held herself together with dignity.

It's been eight years now and we often talk about it because I'm still the only person who does know. Ella confided in me that she often thinks of women who've been through life with an unfaithful husband and the amount of anger and bitterness that won't go away. She says there are times she feels guilty because he's gone, he was taken away from her before she had the chance to give him a piece of her mind. Her last comment to me was: "I suppose the only consolation is that I'll never have to suffer the torture of knowing he's with another woman."

It is important to go with the pain of infidelity, acknowledging it rather than fighting against it. Only when you realize that you need to go with it in order to get over it do you start to heal. Don't try to keep it bottled up inside. That doesn't mean you have to shout it from the rooftops but it does help to con-fide in someone trustworthy. Don't tell yourself that you shouldn't feel the way you do; don't feel guilty and think you're weak or going crazy—it's perfectly normal to feel like this. Going with the pain and acknowledging how you feel is all part of knowing you will get through it, and you will, as impossible as that may seem at the moment.

What infidelity does is make you take a long hard look at yourself, not because you've done anything wrong but because you need to concentrate your attention on you to build a loving relationship with yourself. Never allow what's happened or what may happen to take away the ability to love yourself.

I truly believe that when something like infidelity strikes, then that is exactly what you are meant to deal with at that particular time of your life. In other words, that's your particular lesson to be learned. I can understand that you might be thinking, "I didn't do anything so why do I need to learn a lesson? Surely he's the one who needs to learn something." Yes, you're right but it's obvious from his actions (betrayal) that he isn't learning and you can't make him if he doesn't want to. You are only responsible for your actions so start by working on yourself, and if this has happened before you need to make some conscious changes in your life by learning how to recognize and take responsibility for your part. Remember, we teach people how to treat us, so get really clear about what it is that you want and how you want to be treated and then work on what you are willing to do to create that. Don't expect to get the answers from anyone else because only you know what's right for you.

# Let's talk therapists and counselors

When it comes to dealing with serial betrayers I'm not in the least bit impressed by therapists and counselors. However, there are mitigating factors in that counselors are bound by a strict code of ethics and have to be impartial. Most of my clients are in some form of therapy, live in a fantasyland and are deluding themselves. Throwing rose petals on your partner's pillow at night is hardly going to cut the mustard in a situation as destructive as living with a serial betrayer.

I understand why women keep going back week after week, firstly because at least they feel they are taking an active and positive role by seeking help for their relationship. Don't get me wrong; this isn't a bad thing. In fact, the vast majority of my clients are in need of serious help. It's the kind of help they're receiving that concerns me. Secondly, it is relatively painless and that's why it usually doesn't work.

One of the reasons men have repeat affairs is simply because it's easy. Even if they get caught nothing changes in the long term because so often women give in, give up and accept betrayal as the "for worse" part of their marriage vows they pledged so many years ago. Therefore the betrayer knows exactly what he can get away with. Even if the wife gets her husband to attend counseling there's little chance of the counselor being able to convince anyone who doesn't think they have a problem that they do in fact have one. In fact, he's only there to appease his wife. However, his attending these sessions suggests to his wife the affair must be over, when often it still continues.

In many of the cases I deal with we don't carry out surveillance for clients. They use me as a sounding board for their problems because of my experience in dealing with infidelity, even though they are both in some form of counseling. This often leads them to ask me to meet with and assess their husbands and because I'm not a counselor I can ask (and do ask) the hard questions. With my general experience in dealing with frauds of all types it isn't long into the session before I've sized them up and they know that I know exactly what's going on. This is the point when they can no longer conceal the truth, which is that they're still having an affair while in counseling. The truth of the matter is that these guys have no intention of changing their behavior so they blatantly lie to their wives and counselors.

You don't need to be a brain surgeon to understand that this stuff isn't working. If it was I would see the results in my business, but instead I have new clients every day.

The majority of my clients have been in therapy for years but they aren't facing facts. They're living in a false reality, clinging to the misguided belief that if they go to counseling they'll be able to save their marriage. In reality they can only save themselves and from where I'm sitting I don't even see them doing that.

Life isn't like a textbook. If it were that easy I'd be out of a job, but the truth is I deal with repeat offenders daily. The solution to this epidemic isn't that difficult. It's just that to face what has to be done (which doesn't necessarily mean leaving your marriage) is hard when your heart is involved. Most people intuitively know what they should be doing (you are your own best judge) but so many think they need someone else to tell them how.

When you are seeking professional advice it is important to find someone with beliefs similar to your own. Not all therapists and counselors look down on infidelity. Some even condone it, so it's vital to be in agreement with your therapist in order for them to be able to help you.

One of my clients who sought help from a counselor regarding her husband's continued philandering was told, "Just because you have your boundaries firmly in place doesn't mean you should condemn your husband because he doesn't. You just have to accept that all men play around at some stage."

By all means get some help but never ignore how you are really feeling because only you will know if you are making positive progress. At times like these it is easy to take the soft approach and hear only what you want to hear.

# ten

# MEN ARE THEIR OWN WORST ENEMIES

## Facing the truth

It's a wonder I've got any hair left and haven't pulled it out by the handful in sheer frustration. I know that no one wants to find out their partner has betrayed them, but when the facts are overwhelming and they still continue to come up with excuse after excuse to avoid what is staring them in the face, I often wonder why they called me in the first place. A typical call goes something like this:

CLIENT: "Hi, Julia, my name's Bob and I need your help and advice. Can you tell me if my wife is having an affair?"

JULIA: "Well, Bob, you obviously think something is up so tell me why you feel that way."

CLIENT: "OK, I've been with my partner for about ten years and three months ago she moved out because she said she needed space and now she's living with this guy."

JULIA: "Who is this guy?"

CLIENT: "Oh, he's a friend of hers I've never met, but she says they're just good friends and nothing's going on."

JULIA: "Had she ever mentioned this friend prior to her leaving?"

CLIENT: "No."

JULIA: "Before she left, did you notice any changes in her behavior?"

CLIENT: "Oh yeah, she started taking really good care of herself and buying all this new underwear and our sex life came to a screeching halt."

JULIA: "Did the two of you try to resolve any of your problems? Have you had any counseling?"

CLIENT: "I wanted to have counseling, but when I suggested it she didn't want to know and kept saying she just needed space. I never even knew where she was living until a week ago when my daughter told me and she also told me that sometimes Mommy lies on Graham's bed, but my partner denies everything and I know she wouldn't lie to me. You know, this is killing me because recently she had to have an operation and I went to visit her in the hospital, then later in the day I went back to see her and there was this guy there holding her hand, but when I questioned her later she said he was just trying to keep her awake. Can you tell me if they're having sex? I need to know."

JULIA: "Bob, let's look at this picture so far. You've been in a relationship for ten years and you have a daughter with your partner. She leaves you and moves in with a man she says is a friend but you've never met this friend. She doesn't tell you where she is living and if your daughter hadn't told you I wonder how long it would have been before you found out. She says she needs space so that's not saying the relationship is over yet. She doesn't want to do anything to resolve any issues between the two of you. All this information is telling me that your partner has something to hide. If this man is just a friend, why haven't you met him? After all, he's the male figure around your daughter at the moment, therefore you have a right to know who and what he is. You only found out by chance where your partner and daughter are living and if it is so innocent you should have known from the start. If she needs space one can only presume it's to sort herself out, but then she should be living on her own and actively working on herself, such as getting some professional help, which doesn't seem to be happening."

There is a long silence before the conversation starts again and Bob reveals that his partner and her new friend often go out together on the weekends and on occasions have even gone away together. In essence they're acting very much like a couple but all the time insisting all is above board. All the while Bob is making excuses for his partner. He will explain a situation to me, ask for my opinion, then tell me I'm wrong because his partner's not like that. Every time I answer one of Bob's questions, using all my years of experience, he keeps trying to convince himself he's right by telling me how wrong I am and his partner would never do half of the things he's previously told me she has done.

Are you confused? Well, I am. By the time we end the conversation Bob seems pretty mad at me for telling him the truth as I see it. If someone was to have told Bob this story I'm sure he would have a view very different from the one he currently has. But human nature is such that because betrayal is so painful we will do everything to try and block it out, even when we know it's happening.

Bob's case is not an isolated one and brings to mind another case, that of a guy I call "the apologist" (so much so that this man should have been running his partner's PR campaign).

Chris has actually been a long-standing client and has been involved with Charlene for eight years. The reason for his most recent call is that he found a text message on her phone from another man and now fears losing Charlene because he hasn't married her.

They don't live together but reside in separate towns many hundreds of miles apart and have a number of joint assets. Chris is 15 years older than Charlene and is totally smitten with her, yet they've had problems pretty much from day one. The main issue according to Charlene is that Chris hasn't married her but from his point of view it isn't for the want of trying.

Since his very first phone call to me Chris has related a sorry tale of failed proposals of marriage. Two years into their relationship and on a trip back from Italy Chris produced a two-carat diamond ring and proposed to Charlene while sipping champagne in first class. That was Chris's first mistake. Charlene said that an airplane was an inappropriate place to propose and why hadn't he done it on the beach in Sorrento?

As time went by Charlene started to wear the ring and so Chris, with his hopes raised, asked her where she would like him to propose to her. Her answer was: "Use your imagination, somewhere romantic." Chris whisked Charlene away to the Bahamas and as the vacation progressed she appeared to relax. Chris, feeling that she would now be receptive to a proposal, decided now was the time. Chris made his second mistake when he felt he could kill two birds with one stone by not only proposing but also marrying her while on vacation. But Charlene was having none of his proposal or marriage and pointed out to him that for her to get married she would need the right dress, all the trimmings, with 100 guests. She didn't want to get married on some beach somewhere far from home and her friends and family. From that moment on the vacation was a disaster. Charlene constantly reminded Chris of his failure to get the proposal right, then took the first available flight home, leaving him to ponder his future.

The relationship continued to deteriorate due to Chris's inability (in Charlene's eyes) to get something as simple as a proposal right. As I listened to this I was thinking that any girl would wish for even half Charlene's luck. But everyone's different and Charlene knew just how to play Chris. She had the best of both worlds with Chris supporting her financially and the freedom to come and go as she pleased.

As the relationship deteriorated further Chris was becoming more concerned about Charlene's attitude to his coming to stay as often as he used to. She was becoming downright rude about it. But through all of this Chris was blaming himself for not finding the right place and time to propose when what was really happening was that she was beginning to withdraw from him, even though she still continued to say that everything would be all right once he married her.

During one of our many phone conversations I asked Chris to describe Charlene to me. He gave me all her physical attributes and told me how beautiful she was and how much he loved her and went on to say that though she could have very black moods and did have problems, these were brought on because he hadn't married her. Nothing I said seemed to have any effect. He kept repeating how everything was his fault and how smart, intelligent, witty and charming she could be and what a fantastic personality she had when they were out, how everyone loved her (but no one knew her like he did) and if it wasn't for her black moods and cutting tongue everything would be fine.

I tried and tried to explain to this man that she didn't want to marry him, because if you love someone it doesn't matter where you are proposed to—you're not marrying the proposal, you're marrying the person. Even if Chris went to live with

Charlene I would give him a week and there would be another problem and it would all be his fault. I explained to Chris that he needed to take responsibility for his part in this relationship because as long as he continued to accept responsibility for the guilt Charlene loaded on him she'd keep on using that as a tool to control the relationship the way she wanted it.

This entire situation boils down to the fact that Chris is very insecure and feels that if he took his power back and the relationship finished he would never get anybody as sexy and fantastic as Charlene. Chris is a man living in fear, refusing to face the facts and in doing so will continue to suffer the consequences.

This is a very common pattern I see in both men and women and I call it the "but" syndrome. My clients describe their partners in glowing terms such as the one Chris gave: "She's beautiful, sexy, gorgeous and the most amazing woman I've ever met but. . . ." Or a woman might say about her husband: "He's a wonderful father, husband and provider. He's so good looking and we have so much in common but. . . ."

What these people don't realize is that it's the word "but" which stops these relationships from progressing.

## When men are betrayed

Ask any man and he will tell you that women talk far more than men do. I disagree. Go into any bar and watch men talk about sports: the din is deafening. They can strike up a conversation with a perfect stranger and talk for hours. What men mean when they say that women talk more is not that we actually talk more but that we talk about different things. Men find it unsettling that women can launch into such private areas of their lives without a backward glance, and yet in my business it's men who volunteer so much graphic detail regarding their partners' personal habits, i.e., stains and smells in underwear. The average person wouldn't expect a man to go into such in-depth descriptions (as this is seen as the female domain) nor would they expect men to want these articles of clothing to be forensically tested.

Men call me because it's easier to discuss vaginal secretions with a female than some big burly ex-cop, but then they challenge me about my credentials. Knowing I'm not ex-police they want a full report on my background and qualifications for doing the job. In other words, do I have a degree in snooping?

I'll never forget the look on the face of one of my male investigators when we were out on a case and I got a call in my car. Over the speaker this guy launched into a description of how much discharge he saw each night in his wife's underwear. He was convinced she was having an affair with someone at her work. My investigator sat listening to this and looked like he was in considerable pain. When the call ended he said, "You have got to be kidding me. Does everybody tell you stuff like that?" I replied, "No, only men." The reason for this graphic description is that men don't use their intuition, therefore the evidence has to be something tangible. They approach infidelity in a practical manner and miss the subtle warning signs women are often attuned to. Men become far more desperate and obsessive when it comes to their partners' infidelity. To them it's a sign of their own weakness. Their masculinity and ego are under threat. "How dare she look for another mate when I'm so desirable?"

A noticeable aspect particular to men dealing with infidelity is that by the time they come to me they can be wrong or misguided. I've said many times that when a client comes to me for advice they are 100 percent right. I need to clarify here that I'm talking about my female clients. Because men don't take enough notice of their wives and their daily routines, they will often misread the signs they do pick up on.

Trevor had us follow his wife after finding a garter belt in her underwear drawer that he hadn't seen before. He was convinced she was up to no good during her lunch hour because whenever he asked to meet her she said she was too busy. We followed Trevor's wife as she went window-shopping, and there was one shop she purchased from regularly and that was the fabric store, where she bought elastic, lace and ribbon.

We informed Trevor that in our experience, which came from observing so many people deceiving their partners, his wife wasn't playing around on him. We concluded she was making the garter belts, but Trevor by this stage was totally obsessed and irrational to the point where it was difficult dealing with him. As it turned out we were absolutely correct. She'd been making garter belts for her friend who held "naughty panties" parties. Had Trevor actually listened to his wife he would have known this and if he'd added to this the fact that he'd never had cause for concern before, he would have saved himself the anxiety and stress he put himself through.

# MOST FREQUENTLY ASKED QUESTIONS

Q. If he wants her so much why does he stay with me?

A. Because he doesn't want her more than you, he just wants
her as well as you. If he'd fallen head over heels in love
with this woman and he couldn't live without her then he
might leave you for her as some men do. The ones who
don't are just plain greedy; they want the whole cake, not
just a slice. If you've only recently found out about the
affair then you can see why he hasn't had to leave you because he's been having the best of both worlds without having to make sacrifices such as splitting the assets and losing
face among friends. Mostly these men play and stay because their wives let them.

Q. Is it wrong to have him watched if I suspect him of having
an affair?

A. Absolutely not. Don't ever feel guilty for protecting yourself. As his wife you have every right to know what he's
doing with your health, finances and emotions. I get so angry with women who say they feel guilty about having their
husband watched when they suspect he's betraying them.

Ask yourself, did he feel guilty about disrespecting you, about lying to you and consciously hurting you? No, he didn't, so if you are smart neither will you.

Q. Why does he keep doing this to me? What sort of man is he?

A. He keeps doing it to you because you let him and the only explanation for this sort of man is that he's an uncaring, immature, selfish bastard. A child of four or five wants what he wants when he wants it but a grown man should have learned right from wrong and clearly these men haven't. In fact, I'm doing real men a disservice by calling these guys "men" because quite clearly they aren't.

However if you don't respect yourself you can't expect your husband to. And if you're one of those women who scream and shout but don't take any action, remember you can't keep doing the same thing and expect a different result.

By action I don't mean making him an appointment to see a counselor, because that won't work unless he does it of his own accord. He has to show he's willing to stick it out and not go two or three times and think, "Hey presto! I'm cured." But if he isn't willing to do so and you're not prepared to up the ante, then expect to continue living a life of emotional turmoil.

Q. He's lied to me so much. How can I ever trust what he says again?

A. This is one of the hardest questions to answer because there is no one answer. To learn to trust someone again after something as devastating as infidelity is extremely hard and in some cases impossible. It is such an individual choice and only you will know if you feel truly comfortable with what is being said and done.

If your partner is willing to be completely open and hide nothing from you then in essence he must be completely predictable and be prepared to be patient with you. Then there is a chance for you to restore trust in the relationship. But because we know trust has to be earned it can be a long, long road back and there's no quick fix for infidelity. In fact, it can literally take years to restore trust.

Many men believe that once they have confessed, that should be the end of it and they don't feel they have to do any more.

But let me tell you that unless you know that you've been heard on all levels and your partner has understood the gravity of his immaturity and the choices he's made, then you'll never get over his infidelity. You may as well divide up the assets now.

Q. I know he's having a relationship but is it sexual?
A. Of course it's sexual. Do fish swim? You would have to have rocks in your head to honestly believe that someone engaging in an affair is just going out for coffee or dinner because affairs are all about sex, not sitting around drinking coffee. It doesn't matter if it's looking at either print or Internet pornography, chatting with other women in chat rooms, or having an affair because the end desire is sex. If it was all so innocent then the only question you would have to ask your partner would be, "Would you do any or all of these things with me present?" Then there would be no need for such elaborate lies. If it's not sexual then he should be able to say: "I'm having coffee with such and such a person," and in doing so be comfortable if you were to join them.

The very reason your partner lies to you either blatantly or by omission is because they know what they're doing is wrong. When you ask the question "Is it sexual?" what you're doing is trying to justify your partner's deception and minimize your emotional anguish.

Q. Is it my fault?

A. How can it be your fault if you didn't know it was happening? You didn't give it your stamp of approval so how could you stop it? However, if it has happened before then you have to take responsibility for your part. What you may find is that the reason you ask this question is because your husband has tried to shift the blame by telling you that if you were only more attentive, less busy, slimmer, etc., etc., etc., he would never have done this. Do not take any of that on board. For every action there is a reaction and maybe he should start to take responsibility for his actions.

Q. Why won't he stop when he sees how much it hurts me?

A. The reason he hurts you is because he doesn't care, he doesn't respect you, he's self-centered and selfish. He shows you by his actions how he really feels towards you and no amount of talking can make it otherwise. If you want him to stop, then stand up for yourself. Show him it's not acceptable and mean it.

Q. I think my husband's having an affair but he's at home each evening.

A. This doesn't surprise me because many affairs are conducted during the day. This happens mostly when both parties are married and to go out in the evening would arouse suspicion. However, if the woman is single this is where you may notice the odd late night or even a bogus business trip because she's far more flexible than a married woman. Many clients seem to think affairs are about long languid afternoons together but in my experience they're just snatched moments during the day and it's all over and done with in half an hour. Remember that time isn't the issue here; this is all about sex.

Q. Why won't he tell me the truth? That's all I ask.

A. I wish I had a dollar for every time I've heard this. You'll probably never know the reasons why but in the vast majority of cases the husband is a gutless bastard and his lies are to avoid what he knows will be an unpleasant time if he tells you the truth. He hopes (because it often works) that if he denies and denies it will go away and you'll give up asking. His lies can also be a protection against you in that if he tells you the truth he may feel threatened that you will use the information to undermine him or take control of the relationship. And finally he may fear that there will be far-reaching consequences with family and work colleagues which will damage his image in the eyes of others. When he knows that you know the truth and he still blatantly lies, there is no excuse and no justification and therefore no way you're ever going to be able to make a liar tell the truth.

Q. If I don't catch him in the act won't he just say it didn't happen?

A. You'll probably never get the evidence you think you need (a photograph of your partner in the sexual act) but you will get all the evidence you do need in order to confront your partner and make a decision based on his responses. When it comes to confrontation you must plan carefully what you're going to say. Firstly, you need to clearly identify what information has been gathered and also how your husband's story contradicts what's been said before. If, for instance, your husband has been seen entering a hotel room with a woman at 11 p.m. at night and doesn't emerge until the next day and then, when confronted, denies anything happened and continues to deny, then he's showing you his absolute disregard for you. There's no point in wasting your energies in trying to elicit an honest response.

Q. How can I stop him from continually cheating on me?

A. There is absolutely nothing YOU can do to stop him. Only he can change his behavior—not you. Like I've said many times before: "Leopards don't change their spots and frogs don't turn into princes." If you're living with a serial betrayer the only thing you can do to ensure he doesn't do it again is to remove yourself from the situation.

Q. Why do you need to know who the other person is when it is a 50/50 split nowadays and adultery has gone out of the window as grounds for divorce?

A. Initially, needing to know has nothing to do with money and everything to do with uncovering deceit because no one likes to be lied to and especially not by their spouse. Knowing has everything to do with putting your life back in order and being able to make choices for your future. Uncovering emotional deceit often leads to uncovering financial deceit—for example, the husband has been financially supporting or lavishing gifts and trips on his mistress using joint funds that are not solely his to use. That's when needing to know has everything to do with money.

# TURN THE WOUNDS INTO WISDOM

## Prevention is better than cure

You can't go around giving every new person you meet a lie detector test—as much as you might like to. After you've experienced infidelity it takes time for you to trust yourself in order to trust someone else, and serial philanderers are hardly likely to admit their true nature to you. So in order to protect yourself when you first meet someone it's essential to be a little guarded, especially in the beginning. Ask questions about his past relationships: Has he been married before? What caused his marriage to end? How many serious relationships has he had? Take note of how he answers. If you don't feel comfortable with his answers, don't ignore your intuition. Maybe his friends and family could shed some light. Observe how he behaves when you're out together, especially in female company. A lot of philanderers can't keep their eyes to themselves. We know it is normal and healthy to have an appreciation of the opposite sex but there's a line between appreciation and disrespect for you.

Secrecy is another giveaway for the philanderer but don't confuse secrecy with privacy. Everyone has private zones and that's perfectly normal. Secrets, on the other hand, are issues you must keep hidden or they may have the potential to destroy your relationship. That's why betrayal is always secret. If you have sex with someone outside your marriage then that's not private, that's a secret. It's not about "I can't tell you," it's about "I won't tell you."

Philanderers are more often than not very charming with the gift of the gab and always know exactly what a woman wants to hear. They are usually pretty accomplished in the bedroom department as well but you might well ask if the act is sincere. The answer is no, it's exactly that, an act.

Philanderers have mastered the art of seduction for their own selfish means. They have no regard for anyone else, only for getting what they want when they want and from whomever they can.

Have you ever noticed how quickly people pass judgement on someone, and especially if they are charming and show you even the slightest kindness, that judgement is always a favorable one? Serial killers can have moments of kindness but you wouldn't want to be married to one. Most people will have an opinion and make an assumption on virtually no evidence at all and that's without any form of emotional attachment. So what hope is there for us to be objective when our hearts are involved?

Have you ever heard a woman say after her husband has left her for another woman: "I feel as though I don't even know who he is anymore"? That's probably because she chose to overlook many vital signs and clues to his personality in the beginning. When choosing a mate you need to weigh up all the information as you gather it and see if it corresponds to what you're seeing and hearing. Listen and learn all you can about the object of your affection. Don't feel guilty for doing a thorough job when in fact it's the most sensible approach to take. Look at it as being lovingly suspicious.

When you first meet someone, especially through the Internet, personal ads or contact magazines, you don't have a clue about their emotional or financial history. It's not as though they come with bona fide documents showing you what they say is correct, so you have to trust but be aware. You don't know if this person who has caught your attention has a criminal record, children dotted all over the place, has been abusive to women in the past or is a health risk. You only know what he tells you.

I'm astounded by the number of clients who say to me after the love of their life has betrayed them (either emotionally by cheating or financially by conning them out of thousands of dollars), "He was so charming." Well, he's not exactly going to show you his true colors when he has a hidden agenda, is he?

This is where I'm going to repeat myself. Don't assume that because someone says all the right things in the beginning he must be a good person. Don't take everything you hear at face value, especially when you don't know someone.

When you buy a used car you don't believe everything the salesman tells you because you don't know him and therefore you don't know if he is telling the truth. That's why you get an independent mechanic to check the car over—just to be on the safe side. That's being smart, so why is it that people feel guilty if they even consider doing the same thing to someone they've just met?

I can understand that you might feel all this caution is going against how you were brought up, that is, to treat others as you would want to be treated yourself. Unfortunately, not everyone is like that. That's the problem and one of our biggest mistakes is in believing that they are. The world is a very different place now compared to when our parents were growing up and there are some people who have absolutely no regard for anyone else's feelings. I'm not saying you have to become cynical, because you don't, but if you learn to first look and listen and not just assume, you'll be able to spot pretty quickly someone who isn't on the level. Just be alert and see if there are any clues, because as I've said before, people always show you who they are in the beginning. Never overlook your intuition. Unless it screams at you that you can trust this person, go slowly and take your time.

Making assumptions can often lead to bad judgements. There are certain people in society we automatically look up to because we assume they're worthy of our esteem. Most of us have been guilty of accepting without question the word of doctors, lawyers, priests and judges and anyone in a position of authority. These people have enormous power to abuse because of the simple fact that they appear the least likely. In my line of work I come across many professional men with more kinks than a corrugated-tin roof. Just because someone has achieved a high level of education and learning doesn't make them immune to being emotional deceivers.

There is a raft of questions to be considered before choosing a mate. Here's a good analogy: if you wanted a dog and were a responsible person you would very carefully choose the dog to suit your lifestyle. If you lived in a small inner-city apartment you wouldn't get a Great Dane and if you were a farmer with 5000 head of sheep you wouldn't get a chihuahua as a sheep dog. Instead, you would look for a dog of a suitable size and temperament to suit the situation.

It's not that different when choosing a mate. There are women who will pretend at the beginning of a relationship that they love sports. They'll go with their new partner to the baseball, basketball or football game, when in fact the reason for tagging along is to curry favor with their partner. The minute they're married their interest in sports is turned off like a faucet and they don't go anymore—they've got the guy; they no longer have to pretend. This is misrepresentation and can cause problems further down the track because the guy doesn't have what he thought he was getting. The old adage "Love will conquer all" doesn't appear to be working in the real world. If it were, there wouldn't be the number of relationships in crisis that there is.

Most people have a list of requirements when looking for a mate, but they often overlook the essentials. Some women go shopping for a man with a very limited list of requirements and yet those very same women will shop for a single dress by trying on at least 15 different ones before making a choice. Often, they simply require their prospective partner to have money, power and a university education degree, so I guess that puts Bill Gates out of the running as far as the education goes. Then there are guys who stipulate that the woman they're looking for must be under 30 with no children, so I guess that puts Nicole Kidman out as well.

Can you see how narrow-minded these requirements are and how unrealistic but more importantly how limiting they can be? If we choose our mate on such terms then the narrowness of the criteria must surely increase the chances of us making the wrong choice.

Through my work I find that many women feel like beggars rather than choosers when it comes to finding a mate.

Some feel an enormous relief when anyone shows an interest in them because they've convinced themselves, for whatever reason (maybe they are just lonely or feel too old), that no one is going to want them. They hope to be chosen rather than believe they have the opportunity to choose. What they should be doing is concentrating on what they really want and need at this point in their lives by doing some work on themselves and developing who they are so they don't just get on the bus because it stops at their place.

Make choices for what you want; don't just accept what's there. So many of the women I work for find themselves tied up with deadbeat, drop-kick, good-for-nothing men. These women welcome them into their homes, their hearts, their lives and their bank accounts. They wouldn't normally choose men like this but then they didn't, they just accepted what came along. If you feel grateful to be the chosen one then you can't be particularly choosy. And that's why many of my clients find themselves the victims of emotional and financial fraud.

If you feel a desperate need for an attachment to a man and to be loved, it first has to come from within you. There will always be droughts in your romantic life but isn't it better to tough them out so you know exactly what you want and who you are and know that you don't need a relationship with a man (any man) to make you complete and more fulfilled? This is why many of the women I deal with complain bitterly when they've been deceived because they didn't get to know or really care who he was to begin with. Do you really think the true man of your dreams would want a desperate woman?

The reason 95 percent of my female clients stay in marriages where they have been betrayed is that they just accept betrayal as part and parcel of married life. They stay, truth be told, out of fear, dependency and a desire for security.

Part of the reason for my writing this book is the sheer frustration I feel when I hear over and over again from women whose husbands have lied, cheated, deceived and destroyed them, "But I still love him." Believe me, this isn't love. This is hanging on to a fantasy, a dream of what you thought you had and not what you've ended up with.

I don't think there is a man alive who would tolerate the behavior many of my clients accept. Women will make compromises that can have serious effects on their physical, emotional, mental and financial self for moments of happiness. I am staggered at how intelligent women accept appalling behavior from the man who promised to love and cherish them. Love is about respect, admiration, commitment, honesty and trust, none of which these men are showing these women and yet I keep hearing: "I know he cheated on me and said some terribly hurtful things and will probably do it again, but I still love him."

It's incredible how easily women married to professionals with social standing will endure in silence because they care more about what other people are going to think than valuing themselves. They believe there is a certain social stigma attached to once having been the wife of so and so, and now just being themselves.

I remember reading many years ago about the ex-wife of Roger Moore and how terribly hurt she was because everyone in their old group of showbiz friends ignored her when she was no longer married to Roger. If you put that much value on what other people think I suppose you deserve what you get. It all comes down to this and I can't emphasize it enough: If you don't value yourself, love yourself or put a high enough price tag on yourself then you will only get what you believe you are worth. As the mother of three daughters let me ask you this: Would you want your daughter to have a husband who was a lying, cheating, self-centered, immature, arrogant bastard? You don't have to answer. So why is it OK for you? And why is it OK for you to send the message that it is to your daughters?

There are times when I wish I had a magic wand and could make the hurt disappear but that would defeat the purpose. The hurt is there for a reason and the reason is to teach us a lesson in this lifetime, otherwise we don't grow. I feel this way especially about women I encounter who've been widowed after long marriages and get tied up with a love rat or women whose husbands just up and go off into the sunset with a different model (notice I don't say better or younger because it's not true) after 30 or 40 years together. These women are like inexperienced kids when it comes to distinguishing between romance, love, intimacy and sex.

Elizabeth and Fran, two clients who have confused sex with intimacy, come to mind. Both women were in their sixties and financially secure, and both had nursed their husbands through long illnesses to their final days. What happened in each case is clear. Elizabeth and Fran had very human needs. They needed to be connected to and feel close to someone again. However, these women were confusing what they were getting with what they wanted. Both were married to good honest men and therefore they assumed that because the new men who entered their lives appeared kind and showed interest in them, then they were good men too.

Women fantasize about romance and in their minds they turn a sexual encounter into a romantic one and assume their partner does as well. But as we know, sex for men is often just that, and doesn't include romance, which is exactly what happened here. These two women felt that because their men had sex with them that the relationship had moved to another level of intimacy, but as I pointed out so eloquently, dung beetles have sex so don't go confusing it with anything more than that.

Intimacy is about being able to talk about anything and everything and being able to talk freely about what you're doing, what you want or don't want. When I asked Elizabeth some routine questions about her man, she effectively knew nothing about him although in her mind she felt she did, so much so that she was starting to have thoughts of a long-term relationship.

Women like Elizabeth and Fran probably have more excuse than most for this happening because both came from a generation that simply didn't discuss intimate and personal issues (and especially because younger women today have had more sexual experience). To them sex was a precious gift to be given with love and not something given away casually. They assumed that their new partners understood the value of the gift and felt the same way.

There are plenty of women who jump into bed with someone they hardly know on the first date and then beat themselves up afterwards because they never see or hear from him again. If they took time to clarify a few of the finer points before jumping head first into bed then they wouldn't have to beat themselves up because there would be no misunderstanding and they wouldn't feel used. This behavior is using sex to get love and women do it all the time, and men use this behavior to get sex. Can you blame them if it's gift-wrapped?

The same applied in Fran's case. She allowed sex to happen far too soon, in order to camouflage her feelings of loneliness and her need for closeness. Women like this are starving but they're looking for sustenance from someone else in the form of what they feel is intimacy and caring, but instead it's only sex. The man who came into Fran's life was a con man. The fact he came at all was because Fran called him to clean her windows and the fact she paid him was immaterial in her

eyes because she had romanticized this situation out of all pro-
portion simply because they'd had sex.

Just as women take words far too literally they also take
a man showing sexual interest to mean more than it is. Don't
give sex undeserved power. Yes, it can be fantastic and sub-
lime when it's with the right person but don't use it to fill a
void of emptiness and loneliness in your life because it never
works for longer than the moment lasts.

# Respect, trust, love and commitment

So, in essence, never say never, don't say you will never trust
anyone again or that you will never get involved with anyone
again. Don't lock your heart and happiness away in isolation.
We all have a core purpose for being in this world and as we
journey through life we all have lessons to learn, some harsher
than others—and the wounds of betrayal are deep and painful.

These lessons are there to challenge you because if you
haven't made a mistake and if you haven't had to overcome
obstacles and difficulties in your life then you won't have
learned anything. But having lived through it you now have
survival skills you didn't have before to enable you to protect
yourself if you ever encounter betrayal again.

It's possible to have the joy and passion you deserve in
your life but first you need to have a clear view of what you
want and who you are, not who you think you should be and
not what you think other people expect you to be. Once you
know that, you can then believe in yourself again and learn to
trust. I'm not talking about trusting someone else, I'm talking
about trusting yourself enough to know that you can turn the
wounds into wisdom and cope with anything life throws at
you. You can have the confidence and courage to overcome

any obstacles in your path by having the belief that you can and will ultimately get through it.

Many people live their lives without passion and some even substitute the things that should matter for the superficial, i.e., lots of money, upmarket homes, expensive cars. They constantly seek approval and need to be liked. No amount of money or power makes the man or woman. Learning the lessons and challenging your spirit go a long way to making for a colorful life as opposed to a gray existence. So the next time you're faced with a difficulty think of it only as an opportunity and remember the old adage: "No pain, no gain."

There are four fundamental requirements that are not negotiable when entering a relationship:

## 1. RESPECT

We all know that respect is something to be earned. To be a respectful person is to have character, integrity, principles and compassion. These are qualities you want in yourself and should demand in your mate.

## 2. TRUST

Trust is feeling safe in the knowledge that you can share your vulnerabilities, be totally honest and know you won't be exposed or betrayed in any way.

## 3. LOVE

Love is to care for the feelings of the person we love above our own. It is to honor and hold dear, to take pleasure in and treasure. It is selfless.

## 4. COMMITMENT

Commitment is a pledge, a promise and a covenant not to be broken. It requires loyalty, responsibility and strict adherence to the principles your relationship stands for.

### KEY POINTS

- Don't make the fatal mistake of thinking you can change someone.
- Don't consider someone if you don't like what they show you in the beginning. It will still be there in the end.
- Make sure they have all the physical, emotional, mental, moral and spiritual dynamics you need before you enter into a relationship with someone.
- Finally don't enter into a relationship with anyone you cannot trust or admire.

So to end, my advice is that to be the very best you can be, expect nothing but the very best in return and you will get the best out of life in the future.

# OTHER BOOKS FROM
# ULYSSES PRESS

THE 7 HEALING CHAKRAS:
UNLOCKING YOUR BODY'S ENERGY CENTERS
*Brenda Davies, M.D., $14.95*
*The 7 Healing Chakras* explores the essence of chakras—vortices of
energy that connect the physical body with the spiritual.

ANXIETY & DEPRESSION: A NATURAL APPROACH
*2nd edition, Shirley Trickett, $10.95*
A step-by-step organic solution for preventing anxiety and conquering
depression that puts the reader—not the drugs—in control.

ASHTANGA YOGA FOR WOMEN: INVIGORATING
MIND, BODY AND SPIRIT WITH POWER YOGA
*Sally Griffyn & Michaela Clarke, $17.95*
Presents the exciting and empowering practice of power yoga in
a balanced fashion that addresses the specific needs of female practi-
tioners.

BE YOUR OWN PSYCHIC: TAPPING THE INNATE
POWER WITHIN
*Sherron Mayes, $13.95*
Offers lessons on understanding and programming dreams, acting on
hunches, gaining true insight and following a deeper guidance.

FLIP THE SWITCH: 40 ANYTIME, ANYWHERE MEDITATIONS
IN 5 MINUTES OR LESS
*Eric Harrison, $10.95*
Specially designed meditations that fit any situation: idling at a red
light, waiting for a computer to restart, or standing in line at the
grocery store.

## HOW MEDITATION HEALS: A SCIENTIFIC EXPLANATION
*Eric Harrison, $12.95*
In straightforward, practical terms, How Meditation Heals reveals how and why meditation improves the natural functioning of the human body.

## KNOW YOUR BODY: THE ATLAS OF ANATOMY
*2nd edition, Introduction by Emmet B. Keeffe, M.D., $14.95*
Provides a comprehensive, full-color guide to the human body.

## LOSE THAT LOSER AND FIND THE RIGHT GUY: STOP FALLING FOR MR. UNAVAILABLE, MR. UNRELIABLE, MR. BAD BOY, MR. NEEDY, MR. MARRIED MAN AND MR. SEX MANIAC
*Jane Matthews, $12.95*
This book helps a woman identify the wrong type of man, change negative dating habits and build a relationship that is right for her.

## SECRETS OF THE PEOPLE WHISPERER: A HORSE WHISPERER'S TECHNIQUES FOR ENHANCING COMMUNICATION AND BUILDING RELATIONSHIPS
*Perry Wood, $12.95*
The author shows how the same techniques for developing trust and understanding with a horse can work equally well in one's personal, business, family and romantic relationships.

## YOGA IN FOCUS: POSTURES, SEQUENCES AND MEDITATIONS
*Jessie Chapman     photographs by Dhyan, $14.95*
A beautiful celebration of yoga that's both useful for learning the techniques and inspiring in its artistic approach to presenting the body in yoga positions.

*To order these books call 800-377-2542 or 510-601-8301, fax 510-601-8307, e-mail ulysses@ulyssespress.com, or write to Ulysses Press, P.O. Box 3440, Berkeley, CA 94703. All retail orders are shipped free of charge. California residents must include sales tax. Allow two to three weeks for delivery.*

# ABOUT THE AUTHOR

**Julia Hartley Moore** is New Zealand's and Australia's most recognized private investigator, despite having left school at age 14. A year after leaving school, Julia had her first child, and by the age of 16 had three children under the age of 1. By the age of 19 she was separated, then divorced two years later. In the intervening years Julia raised her three daughters, married and divorced her multimillionaire second husband, and worked as an in-house model and for Mohammed al-Fayed at Harrods in London. In 1995, without any formal police background, Julia became the first woman to own a private investigation company in New Zealand.

She has been featured in numerous documentaries including *Documentary New Zealand*, *60 Minutes* and *Today Tonight Australia*, and appears on New Zealand and Australian television and radio shows. Julia is a regular columnist for women's magazines, and is sought after by the media for her expert advice and commentary on human nature, relationships and infidelity issues. She lives in New Zealand. For more information on Julia, visit her website: www.juliamoorepi.co.nz.